How to be Greek without being Greek

A guide to Greece (and living life)

How to be Greek without being Greek

A guide to Greece (and living life)

By **Tom Simek**

Cover photograph: Dan Simek
Cover design: Lara Melachrinou Simek
Sketches: Tom Simek

21, Ioannou Ralli str., 14452 Metamorphosi Attiki,
210 3306880, 210 3610519, 210 2855183

ISBN 978-960-394-810-0

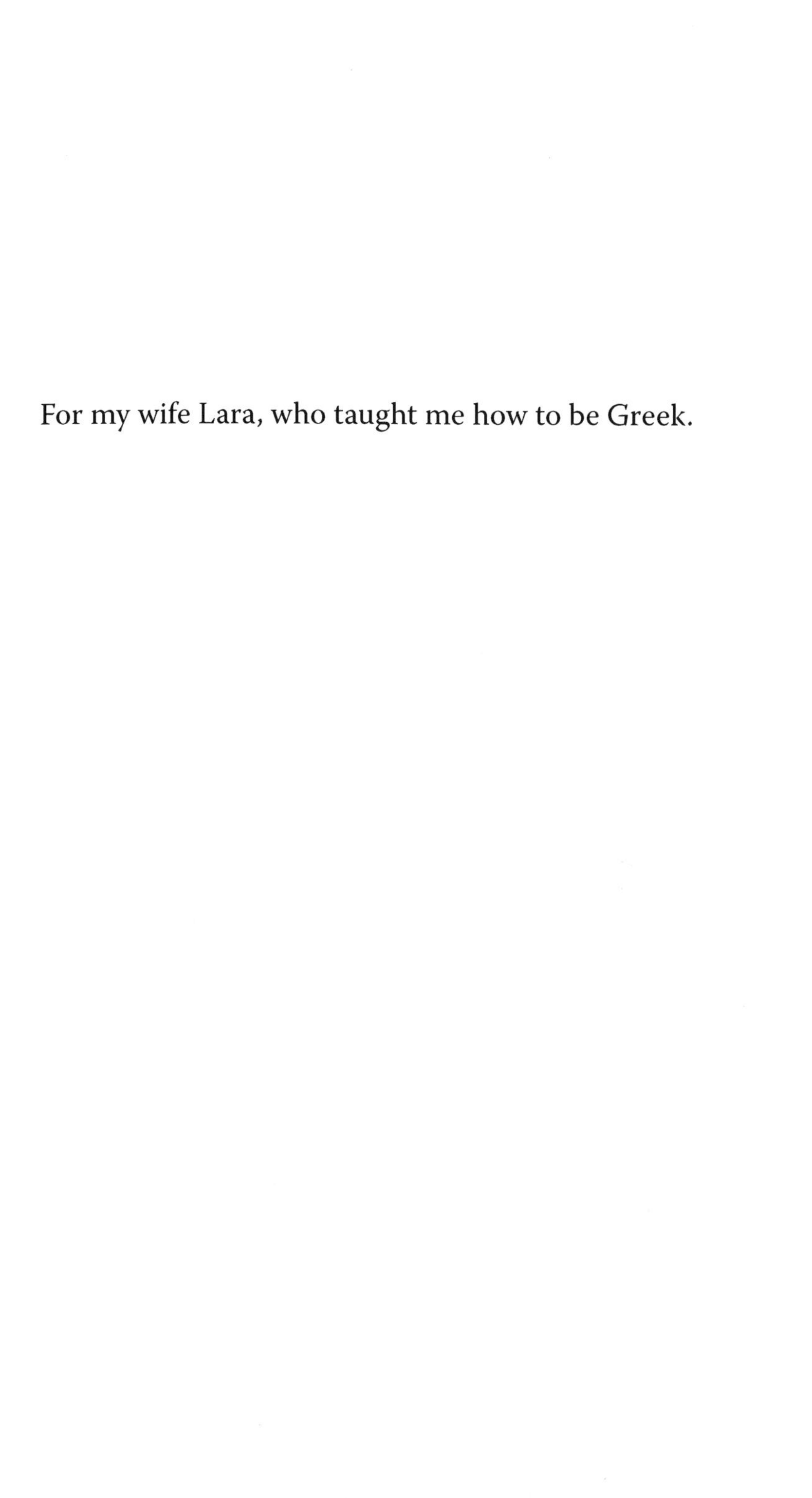

For my wife Lara, who taught me how to be Greek.

Table of Contents

Introduction: A (very) brief history

Democracy. Science. Theatre. Philosophy. Education: All products of Greece, born on the shores of the Mediterranean, just like Socrates, Pythagoras, and Alexander the Great. Greeks are as keen mentally, as they are strong physically and I've even heard it said that Greeks are the smartest people on Earth. They could rule the world, if they wanted to (or so the joke goes), but they'd rather sit around and drink coffee instead.

Greeks have a long history of being relaxed, and their chilled out way of life is most likely due to their environment, which is extremely favorable to human inhabitation. The climate is mild and besides the mountainous interior, the temperature along the coast seldom ever gets below freezing. There's a lot of sunshine, a decent amount of rain and natural springs full of mineral water, natural resources, which make basic survival pretty easy since food can be cultivated year round and all the shelter you really need is a roof overhead. It's no wonder that people started permanently settling these lands tens of thousands of years ago, because it was and simply is a great place to live.

Although the summer months can get sweltering, relief from the heat is never far away. The bountiful blue sea provides a steady wind and cool waters, which are both refreshing and rich with marine life. The sea's bounty of fish and invertebrates provides all of the protein necessary to fuel the human brain (a task that many cultures still struggle with even today).

With their basic needs met, the Greeks were able to mature quickly and made their token attempt at world domination five hundred years before Rome, when most other people were still just trying to figure out how to stay alive. The Greeks found out the hard way, way back then, what happens to empires and they see no need now to have another go at it again. Because unlike the British, who are stuck on a cloudy, rainy island and forced to colonize other lands to make up for their own lack of natural resources, the Greeks have pretty much everything they truly need right here at home. They live in the same place they vacation, so even now, in the modern world, they can't find much of a reason to go anyplace else. Why travel? They're already where everyone else in Europe comes to party.

Greece is not new to hosting visitors. Its location at the crossroads of civilization made it a convenient center point for trade and commerce around the Mediterranean, and the influx of people "just passing through" made it ripe for social advancement, as many products and enlightening ideas traveled through its borders. However, its central seat amidst conflicting cultures has also brought Greece much turmoil, and throughout its long history, Greece's glory has been equally matched with misery, as Greece has been subject to numerous invasions and occupations by foreign entities.

The Ottoman Empire, or "the Turks," occupied the Greek peninsula for nearly four hundred years, ending only fairly recently (in historical terms), during the first half of the19th century. Over those four long centuries, the Greeks faced enormous hardships and cultural oppression at the hands of their closest neighbors. They were forced to live as second-class citizens on their own native soil and for a third of a millennia they had no basic rights or freedoms. Even their own native tongue was forbidden to speak. Yet with patient defiance and an eventual grassroots revolution, the Greeks somehow managed to secretly preserve their language and their culture, passing it on clandestinely and keeping it alive subversively for more than fifteen generations.

Mind over matter. Work smart, so you don't have to work hard. Steal from the government. That's the Greek way. Even if they've never had the numbers, they've always found a way to win wars. Even now, despite being such a tiny country, everybody in the world still seems to be talking about Greece. It has a certain power because it holds a strong history. Every western democracy is built off of its legacy and all western written language is derived from Greek. Many of the words they used, we still use today.

The Greeks are the ones who seemingly started it all. They really got the ball rolling for the modern world. They created mathematics and logic, and philosophical ideas about existence and our place in the universe. They came up with the whole idea of the human epic. Greece is home to the gods and mythological men, like Ulysses and Achilles, legendary both for their strength and achievements, as well as their mistakes and their flaws. But it was really innovation that secured the Greeks their place in history.

The Athenian Empire was unique from the get go. Most other empires at the time were monarchies built around some sort of fertile plain, which offered the land necessary for large-scale agriculture and in turn huge populations and massive armies. Athens, on the other hand, was a democracy built on rocky and rugged terrain. It never housed an enormous population or vast armies (when compared to other empires before and after it). Yet the Greeks still somehow managed to exert their influence all over the world, even to this day. How? How did they manage to do it? How did they make so much out of so little? How did they cast such a big shadow while being so small?

The answer is simple. The Greeks are creative. They managed to unlock the potential of the human mind and, acting in the true spirit of homo sapiens, they did what nobody else had done before them. They were no different, as people, than anyone else, but they allowed themselves to be free and therefore did things in ways others didn't. Athens was the first real meritocracy, which built its wealth by using ingenuity and invention.

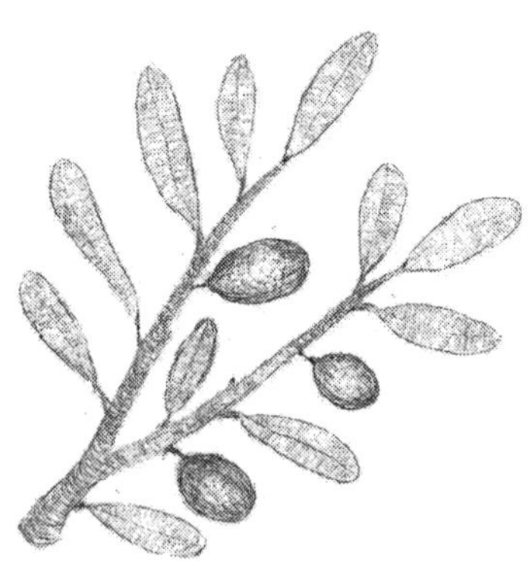

Olives have become synonymous with Greece and there's a good reason for it. Olives grow everywhere in Greece. They are really the only leafy-tree with edible fruit that can grow wild in the soil and survive the harsh summer sun. Like the Greeks themselves, olives are resilient and strong, and it's what's hidden inside those olives that originally made the Greeks so rich.

Oil, of all kinds, has been a precious resource throughout human history. Even to this day, wars are waged over it. But before there was petroleum to power combustion engines and whale oil to light lamps, there was grease to cook with. Traditionally, people used animal fat, but the Greeks, always using their minds, figured out a way to effectively and efficiently extract the oil out of vegetables. And in the process of doing so, the Greeks discovered a resource more useful and precious than gold. Economically, it was cheaper to create and the health benefits were merely a bonus, seemingly rewarding their ingenuity. To me, it's really no coincidence that "Greece" is called "Greece," although it should really be spelled "Grease." (Note: this is not really the reason why Greece is called Greece. The name was derived from the term "Graeki," which was what Latin speakers called people that came from the region that is now Greece.)

Furthermore, the Greeks capitalized by simply taking advantage of what was already around them: the sea and the wind. They built the strongest and fastest sailboats to move their product and patrol their seas. As it turned out, with a little creativity, the Greeks found the perfect set up in conditions, which seemed less than ideal. Being already almost impossible to attack by land, all Athens had to do was create a technologically unmatched navy. They ruled their empire by controlling all of the ports, that way they didn't need large numbers of foot soldiers or to sustain massive occupying armies They just needed tactical strategy.

So in a world entirely ruled by monarchies and oligarchies, the Greeks blossomed into a democracy almost 2,500 years before the rest of Europe started to dethrone their kings. And Ancient Greece was a true democracy, unlike the republics we live in today. As opposed to voting for representative officials in a government, the citizens of Athens held a debate and voted directly on the issues, with no middlemen involved.

Each citizen got one vote that they could cast on any civil proposal presented, ranging from creating and repealing laws to declaring war. Willing participants gathered at the base of the Acropolis and cast their ballots of either a white stone, signaling yes, or a black stone, signaling no. The Greeks even had a clever means to protect their fragile democracy against tyrants and power hungry citizens.

Once a year, they cast a vote with a rather peculiar result. Each citizen scrawled the name of a person onto a piece of tile and whoever's name appeared the most was thereby banished from Athens. It was a way of deterring dictatorial behavior and preventing any citizen from becoming too strong. The tiles they cast were called "ostrako" and is where the word "ostracize," meaning to cast out, comes from.

But like all people, the Greeks are not without their faults. Athens almost went bankrupt numerous times, most notably when building the Acropolis, which served both as a temple for the goddess Athena and a citadel for protection against enemy attack. Besides its spiritual purpose, the Acropolis's functionality as a fortress and practical worth was highly controversial back then and is still debatable today, as the structure could house the entire population of Athens, but could do nothing to protect their resources or withstand a long siege. And like every empire, the greatest enemy turned out to be the self.

Athens ended up falling largely as a result of its own foolishness. The Greeks lost control. The empire got too big and essentially imploded upon itself. The proud and overly ambitious military leaders lost sight of what had originally made it great and the mighty civilization collapsed rather quickly after overextending its military and squandering most of its wealth to fight unneeded, greed-fueled wars in far off places, while all the time leaving its home front to rot and vulnerable to attack.

Poetically, the end of Athens can be seen to coincide with the death of one its most famously intelligent citizens, Socrates. At the height of its greatness, Athens was full of "philosophers," sometimes geniuses who roamed the streets barefoot, teaching, debating and arguing with each other. These visionaries held no possessions and declared work to be a morally degrading waste of time.

In the hustle bustle of today's commerce driven, "time is money" society, those free thinkers would have easily been considered bums. But Socrates figured out something that most overly ambitious don't ever seem to learn: sometimes, nothing is the best thing you can do. The idea applies not only to doctors and philosophers, but to interpersonal relationships, parents and military commanders as well.

Amidst great prosperity, men, like Socrates, were given the opportunity to just sit around and do nothing. And they took advantage of that opportunity, not for themselves, but for all posterity to come. Ironically, the modern world was born out of their inaction. It was only when people let their minds roam free that they actually started to analyze, to invent and to dissect the physical and metaphysical world. If people like Socrates, Plato and Pythagoras had been made to work the fields, they would have never contributed what they did to Athens or to humanity. So in essence, they accomplished more by doing nothing than most people do working their entire lives.

Socrates, in particular, was more than just a lazy bum and his influence stretches far beyond theoretical philosophy into the socio-political arena because Socrates was, in a sense, the world's first famous martyr. He often spoke out publicly against conventional wisdom and logically questioned the practicality and validity of political and military proposals. However, it wasn't this vocal dissent that actually got him killed. It was his radical teachings.

Socrates was forced to drink poison for ideas, which critics claimed were poisoning the minds of the youth in Athens. All Socrates had to do was stop teaching and recant his claims, and his life would have been spared. But instead of rebuking those controversial ideas and thus prolonging his life, Socrates stubbornly, and in true Greek form, chose integrity over death, thereby sealing his fate as a saint in the community of freethinkers. Socrates' methods of critical thinking, peaceful civil disobedience and passive defiance in the face of violent oppression made him a predecessor to the world's most transformational figures, like Mahatma Gandhi and Martin Luther King. But what makes Socrates' case so unique is that he didn't die trying to accomplish any singular goal or further some specific cause. He had nothing to gain or to lose by what he was saying. He just said it because he thought it was true and needed to be said. So Socrates was essentially a martyr for nothing more (and nothing less) than truth itself.

You could say that with Socrates' forced suicide, the Ancient Greek society metaphorically killed itself, commencing its own decline by censoring that same freedom of thought, which had originally made it prosper. The action backfired, because not only did Socrates' death rob the Athenians of a brilliant mind, it only served to incense and solidify his followers, who further spread his message and kept his ideas alive until today.

Likewise, many aspects of Socrates' tragic story still ring true about modern Greek society: Socrates inaction and bull-headedness, the Greek authority's uncompromising lack of foresight and its habit of only making problems worse. The Athenians have burned down their own city multiple times just to deter and spite their invaders and the Greek government seems to be perpetually bankrupt.

The Greeks are overall pretty laid back and relaxed. Some might even call them lazy and surely many are. But no matter how lazy a Greek might be, one thing is for sure: if a Greek doesn't like something, you're surely going to hear about it (even if they might not actually do anything to change it.) All of the strikes and public protests, which are a routine occurrence in Athens, merely reflect that history of defiance stemming from Socrates. The citizens' demands are hardly ever met and the protests seldom accomplish anything. The authorities usually just make some minute concession to stop the people from yelling and breaking things, but in the end, nothing actually changes.

Greeks are loud and their loudness, even when casually talking to each other, is something that most foreigners have to get used to. If you don't understand Greek, it may seem like they're always fighting, but in reality, they're not. They're usually just shooting the breeze with a friend. It's not yelling. It's just the way they talk. They're passionate people. After all, the Greeks did invent drama.

Chapter lessons:

- All you really need is food, water and shelter. You can't progress without securing those first.
- The mind is the most powerful tool and weapon. Use it. Don't lose it.
- Be creative.
  - Make the most out of what you've got.
  - Don't let mundane business consume your thoughts.
  - Entertain the impossible and impractical.
  - Just because nobody has done it, doesn't mean it can't be done.
- Sometimes you can accomplish more by doing less.
- The world cannot be conquered by force.
- All empires will fall.
- Hold truth above all else.

How to...

Going for Coffee

This is one aspect of Greek life that stands out above all the rest and from the number of Greeks you'll see sitting at cafeterias at two-thirty on a Wednesday afternoon, you might think it's all they ever do. Going for coffee is a cornerstone of Greek social life. Some Greeks go multiple times a day, everyday and most Greeks will go at least once a week, and at weekends. Really, it's just an excuse to get out of the house and catch up with friends. But it's also the place to have meetings and talk business informally. It's the place you go for your first date (it's how my wife and I started), and it's something you do for any occasion or for no reason at all.

Going for coffee is not to be taken lightly and if you choose to go with a Greek, you have to know that you're in for a good two to three hour activity, because cafeterias function as much more than a place to get coffee. Coffee, like alcohol, merely serves as a social lubricant for interacting, meeting people and showing off.

The coffee is outrageously priced and it might be the most expensive cup of coffee you've ever drunk. But you are paying for much more than the coffee. You are paying for the atmosphere and to occupy a table for a good portion of the afternoon. Anyone who thinks a cup of coffee is just a cup of coffee will be quickly overwhelmed by the number of options you can choose from in Greece. So here is a brief guide on what to drink and how to drink it.

Most of the coffees are variations on Italian and French models. There is really only one "Greek Coffee," but it's actually Turkish. First off, the coffees can be broken down into two main categories: hot and cold. During the sizzling summer months, the last thing you'll probably want to drink is a steaming cup of coffee. Therefore, cold coffee is usually a more popular choice during July and August, but also remains a standard for warm days throughout the year.

There are two main types of cold coffees: "a freddo" and "a frappe." "Freddo" is Italian for "cold" and has two subcategories, based on the most popular types of Italian coffee: the cappuccino and the espresso. A "freddo cappuccino" and a "freddo espresso" are exactly as the names suggest.

Figure 1

A "freddo cappuccino" (Figure 1) is an iced cappuccino, a strong brew of coffee topped with steamed milk, while a "freddo espresso" is simply that same strong coffee, iced, but without the steamed milk. A "frappe," (Figure 2) on the other hand, is essentially just instant coffee whipped into a froth, to which ice, water and milk (if you choose) are added. Cold coffees, like most coffees, can be taken in three ways: sweet, medium, or "sketo" (meaning "without"), depending on how much sugar you want.

A "Greek coffee" is a strong, hot coffee, made by boiling grounds directly in the water. So if you order a Greek coffee, you

Figure 2

have to let it sit for a couple of minutes before you drink it, in order to let the coffee grounds in the water sink to the bottom. Afterwards, you'll see a filmy residue, which you don't want to drink, at the bottom.

You can also have a standard filtered coffee, which is called "a French coffee" in Greece, or you can choose to take a hot espresso or hot cappuccino in a single or double (diplo) serving. Decaffeinated coffee is not something you generally see (because really, what's coffee without caffeine). However, if you are truly not a fan of coffee, most cafes also offer a wide variety of beverages, from tea to hard alcohol to fresh juice.

You won't have to go far to find a café because they are literally everywhere in Greece, but, in my opinion, if you want to have the true Greek coffee experience, then you have to pick a café that is packed with people and drink one of the cold coffees.

When at a café, you needn't wait for a host. Just sit down at any free table and once sitting, a waiter will bring you two things: a glass of water and an ashtray. Select the type of coffee you'd like and remember to tell them how sweet you want it (sweet, medium or sketo). That part is easy enough, it's drinking it that's the tricky part.

You see, in Greece things move slowly and that's exactly how you should drink your coffee. Slowly and I don't mean just slowly. I mean incredibly slow, like you drink hard liquor, no faster than the ice melts.

For non-Greeks, this is usually a bit of a challenge, so if you're with a Greek, use restraint and let them set the pace. If you must set your own tempo, it might be helpful to think of it as a little game. Who can drink their coffee the slowest? It should take at least an hour to finish a cup of coffee and even then, you're still drinking way too fast. **So here are few more tips on how to slow down and drink coffee "the Greek way."**

- Drink the water to help pace yourself.
- Cold coffees must be drunk with a straw. (Seriously, they'll always give you one). Use it to take tiny sips and mix the coffee around from time to time.
- It helps if you're a smoker, because cigarettes just seem to go with coffee and smoking gives you something else to do. If you do smoke, smoke freely. There's no shame in lighting one cigarette off up another.
- Talk, a lot. That's what Greeks do.
- Constantly check out other people in the café and passers by. It's part of the show.
- You can also order a toasted sandwich or a bite to eat, but under very few circumstances should you order another coffee. That's for advanced drinkers. If you're an amateur, it's perfectly ok to have a second or even third coffee, but you should move to another cafeteria first. It's like an unwritten rule.

Eating Souvlakia

Probably the next biggest aspect of Greek life, after drinking coffee, is eating souvlakia. Souvlakia can be made from a wide-variety of grilled meat and, like coffee, contain many subtle variations of basically the same thing. The Greeks love to eat and although they do eat a lot of fish and vegetables, they like nothing more than fatty, greasy, grilled meat.

If you're a vegetarian, this aspect of Greek life might be your hell, as there is usually a strong smell of grilled meat wafting through the air outside every tavern. But animal lovers can rest assured that the animals are usually treated humanely. They are not raised on gigantic corporate farms. Most are graze-fed and herded on the free-range, so the animals live a happy life and as a result produce very good meat.

No matter which type of souvlakia you choose, you're also going to eat at least three other things along with it: pita, fried potatoes and tzatziki. Pita is the traditional Greek flatbread, which is dipped in olive oil and grilled. Fried potatoes are what the British call "chips" and the Americans "French fries," and tzatziki is the traditional yogurt-garlic-cucumber sauce, which Greeks eat with almost every food.

The two main choices of souvlakia depend on what type of meat you want and how you want to eat the pita. The meat is broken down into two categories, the "kalamaki" and the "gyro " (pronounced YEE-ro, with a throaty "g"). Kalamaki literally means "straw" but refers to skewered chunks of pork or chicken, which are grilled. It is essentially what other Westerners call "a kebab." (Although in Greece a kebab is something else.)

Gyro meat, as the word "gyro", meaning to "spin" or "turn" suggests, comes from a large spit of shredded chicken or pork, which is slowly rotated on a vertical axis and cooked from the outside with radiant heat. As the meat gradually browns, the outside layer is shaved off, yielding bite-sized, slightly singed, greasy pieces of heavenly goodness.

After you have chosen which type of meat you want, pork or chicken, then you must choose how you want to eat it. You can take the meat sketo (without) and just eat pita on the side, or take a "pita kalamaki" or a "pita gyro." These are succulent sandwich-like wraps stuffed with onions, tomatoes, fried potatoes, and tzatziki, along with the meat of your choice. Depending upon what tavern you are at, one of those pita wraps can be enough to fill you up, but to make it more of a meal, you generally also take a portion of fried potatoes and maybe a salad as well.

The typical Greek salad is called a "horiatiki," or a "village salad," since "horio" means "village" in Greek. A horiatiki contains no lettuce, but is instead based around cube-sliced tomatoes mixed with cucumbers, onions, green peppers, olives and a slice of feta on top. Feta is a soft, salty cheese derived from goat's milk, and is another one of Greek's most famous staple foods.

The horiatiki is typically dressed with olive oil and sometimes vinegar. Then finished off with dried oregano and salt sprinkled on top. The salad often comes undressed or maybe with just a touch of olive oil. Therefore, it is generally up to you to add the vinegar and salt to your taste. Salt is another mainstay of Greek cuisine and is used quite liberally with everything. So if you have high blood pressure, be careful about adding more, since there is usually a lot already in the food.

Tips for eating souvlakia at a tavern:

- It's ok to eat with your hands. (Really, there's no other way.)
- Plates are usually shared, family style.
- Drink beer or the house wine, which comes from a barrel and is served in a carafe. It's usually decent and cheap.
- Don't plan on kissing anybody after you eat tzatziki, unless they have eaten tzatziki too, because it makes your breath reek so fierce of garlic that you become immune to vampires.
- There are usually toothpicks right on the table. Trust me, you're going to need them.

Drinking Ouzo

Ouzo is probably the most famed alcoholic beverage produced in Greece. It is distilled from grapes and is an anise-flavored liquor, which tastes a bit like liquorice and is often compared to its Italian counterpart, sambuca. Like drinking coffee, imbibing ouzo is a delicate process with its own protocol as to how it is done.

First off, ouzo is always served on the rocks, ice-cold, and with a splash of water (how much water depends on how strong you like it). The clear liquid turns a cloudy-white when mixed and is perfect for sipping on the shores of the sea during the summer. However, take caution and drink responsibly because ouzo goes down very smoothly. Don't let the soothing taste fool you. Ouzo is a hard-liquor and contains the same amount of alcohol as a typical vodka or whiskey. So it's very easy to go overboard without even thinking, especially when sitting in the hot sun. This is why certain precautions must be taken when drinking ouzo.

The most important rule is never drink ouzo alone or by itself. You always have to be with somebody and to eat something while you're drinking it, whether it is a full dinner or just some crisps and nuts. Ouzo should be sipped slowly and, like coffee, savored for hours. If you do it right, you can ride a nice happy buzz all evening, without ever getting full-blown drunk.

Ouzo generally goes with most foods but fits particularly well with seafood, like calamari and octopus. A solid option is to drink it with a "pikilia," a mixed plate of food that most restaurants offer. A "pikilia" usually contains a variety of appetizers, from dips to grilled meat. You can usually choose the size of a pikilia (for either two or four people), but each restaurant offers its own variation, so ask what's in it first and don't expect to get the same "pikilia" everywhere.

Beyond that, here are some general directions on how to properly imbibe ouzo:

- Use a tall, skinny glass
- Fill the glass almost completely with ice
- Slowly pour the ouzo over the ice, filling it about ¾ full
- Top it off with water
- Sip and enjoy while snacking (Note: unlike iced coffee, do not drink ouzo with a straw!)

Other highly traditional Greek alcohols that you might like to try are "raki," "tsipouro" and "mastika." All are similarly derived from grapes and produced as a by-product of wine (or juice), utilizing the solid remains of the fruit. Raki is essentially an unflavored variation of ouzo and tsipouro is yet another form, which is often served warm and with a touch of honey (making it perfect for winter.) Finally, mastika has a distinctly sweet taste, being flavored by the resin of a small pine tree, which is grown mainly on the island of Chios.

Going to the beach

Even though there are a countless number of beaches scattered all over Greece, everybody seems to want to go to the same ones, which get packed to the point where you're basically sitting on top of each other. This is partially due to accessibility and population distribution, but also has to do with the quality of beaches, which vary greatly in Greece. Not all beaches are created equally and some are just much, much better than others.

Some of the beaches are sandy, while others are rocky. Some have warmer water and some are dirty. Even a single beach's enjoy-ability factor can seriously fluctuate from day to day depending on what time you go and which direction the wind is blowing. Beyond that, there are certain beaches that are just "cool" and others that are not. The other reason for the crowdedness, besides topography, is that Greeks are an urban people. It's in their blood. They live centrally in cities and don't like to feel like they're alone. Even if someplace is already overcrowded, they're going to pack themselves in as tightly as they can, instead of going someplace else that might have less people.

So, in a sense, going to the beach is something like going for coffee and in fact, going to the beach usually entails having a coffee, because hey, why not? And because the beach is social, that also means you've got to look good. The general rule in Greece is dress to impress and at some beaches, that means more than just an expensive, brand name bathing suit. Some Greeks go to the beach dressed like full on divas: make-up, high heals, and a big hat. Typically a t-shirt and a nice pair of shades will do, especially if you're young and have a good body, which many Greeks do. So the beach can also be a great place to kick back, relax and admire the human form.

In the summer, the sun is extremely strong from 11 a.m. until 4 p.m. So the beaches tend to get crowded later rather than earlier, both because it gets so hot and because Greeks like to do things late and in their own time anyway. If you're really looking for a place to relax and have your own space, then you're going to have to travel and look pretty hard, because most of the good beaches are crowded and have some sort of beach bar thumping dance music.

Technically, you cannot own a beach in Greece and besides a few of the beaches around Athens, where the town charges a fee, all beaches in Greece are free and open to the public. The beach bars and hotels get permission to put out chairs and umbrellas, which they can and will charge you to use. Young and attractive waiters provide service and encourage you to purchase something, at least a coffee or a drink when you sit down. So like most things in Greece, the beach usually ends up turning into a party, since there is already loud music and plenty of drinks.

At the most popular beaches, you have to make a reservation for an umbrella, but if you don't want to pay, you can usually find a place to sit down on your towel. But remember, if you're looking to make an impression, sitting on your towel is just not as cool as paying for a spot under an umbrella. Plus, the umbrella can be well worth the price just for the small amount of shade it offers, especially if you intend on staying at the beach for a couple of hours. You usually don't bring your own food or drink, because it's a pain in the heat and there's always someplace to buy something. (Besides, bringing your lunch just isn't cool either.)

Once you stake a claim on your spot, it's yours for the day. But don't leave it, or you will lose it and be careful when you go for a swim, or to the bathroom, because thieves are common on beaches, as they are in much of Greece.

Games and horseplay on the beach are as ordinary as sunbathing and swimming. Volleyballs are normally being knocked around in the water among groups of people and many Greeks, not just children, will spend much of their day playing "racquets." Racquets is a game like "paddleball," in which solid wooden paddles are used to quickly knock a tennis ball back and forth between two or more people. So amidst the already crowded atmosphere, there are often numerous tennis balls whizzing around, further adding to the chaos.

As the sun sets, the music gets turned up and some beaches turn into an outdoor club. The Greeks love to dance, however, take note. If you're on an island and see groups of people getting naked, completely wasted and doing lots of crazy, stupid stuff, they're most likely foreigners and not Greeks. Each summer, millions of sexually charged, blossoming teenagers flood into Greece from England, Italy, and the rest of the world to wreak havoc on their first vacation away from their parents. Obnoxious tourists are a necessary discomfort the Greeks are forced to put up with, and although the Greeks love showing off their country, they despise rude foreigners who come in year after year and act like barbarians in their home.

My only tips for going to the beach are pretty basic:

- Put on plenty of sunscreen.
- Be careful of thieves.
- Bring something to do. Besides reading material or a game, a pair of goggles can be handy, since the beautiful, clear water is perfect for snorkeling.
- And finally, a warning: Don't be "that guy" who gets so drunk by five o'clock that he ends up passing out in the sun or making a complete fool out of himself in broad daylight.

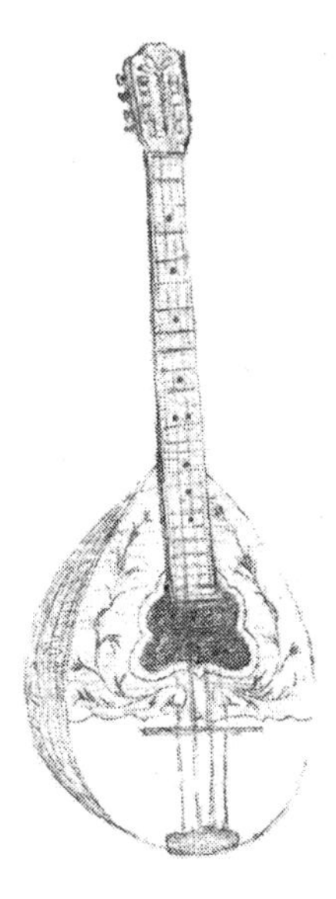

Bouzouki

Another place to go out and show off is in the Greek music clubs. Music of all different kinds is a huge part of Greek life, and although they're not the biggest fans of classical music, the Greeks love pop, rock, blues, R&B, electronic, hip hop and pretty much anything you can dance to.

Greece has a wide array of its own traditional folk music, which is unique to each different region. The rhythm of Greek music, in general, is quite complex and can be hard to follow, but much of it is set for dance.

"Bouzouki" (shown on the left) is actually the name of an eight-stringed instrument (containing 4 pairs of double strings) that is plucked with a pick, like a guitar, and looks like a loot with a long neck. But "bouzouki" is also the name used for the style of music, which the bouzouki is used to play, as well as for the name of the clubs where that style of music is performed.

Lots of people can end up spending an entire week's salary during one night at a bouzouki club. So, needless to say, like most things in Greece, it can be expensive. There is usually a cover charge to get in, and in order to reserve a table, or anyplace to sit down, you must make a reservation and also buy a bottle of alcohol, which can cost anywhere from a hundred euros and up. However, for the money, buying a bottle usually turns out to be more economical than everyone ordering drinks independently, since the drinks themselves are expensive and you usually don't end up going out for just one drink.

Bouzouki clubs offer an entire night of live music and entertainment (usually from about 11 p.m. until 6 a.m.) featuring a house band and a complete line up of singers, which usually contains one or two known, pseudo-famous singers, who rotate, taking turns singing solo and duets together. Most Greek singers become famous singing in bouzouki clubs, and even the most famous Greek singers today still sing in bouzouki clubs, because the pay is extremely good.

Along with the standard bouzouki music, the band often plays covers of popular English and American pop songs, as well as "endechno," which is essentially artsy Greek rock. The clubs usually get pretty heated and end up with the entire crowd singing along to the well-known songs, while people dance around in circles and even get up on top of the tables.

The clubs are fancy and, like cafeterias and beaches, are also places where you normally get dressed up to go and strut your stuff. Besides all of the expensive food and drinks the Greeks may order, another thing they do to show off and literally "throw" their money away on is buying carnations. For a pretty penny, you can purchase a basket of carnations, which are not meant to be given to your girl or taken home, but rather thrown up onstage, as both a show of one's affection for the singer and one's generosity.

The comical thing is that the clubs sometimes have people going around and picking up all of those flowers, which they resell again and again. So the people essentially buy back the same expensive flowers they just threw on the ground, only to throw them away again. But this silliness is also the point, being a social platform to receive attention and tastefully flaunt one's wealth in a public setting. It doesn't matter if you're actually rich, because in Greece, as in the world in general, image is everything. So this trivial display can be an easy way to score points with anyone you might be trying to impress.

Overall, the Greeks are big fans of going out to see live music. DJ's are popular for the "real clubs," but there are also music clubs for all types of rock and R&B, which target a younger and less traditional audience wanting to go out, but not to bouzoukia. So the music scene in Greece is alive and extremely vibrant, despite being such a small country, and since there is such a large audience willing to patronize live music, large music festivals occur frequently, and most major musical acts make Athens a yearly stop on their European tour. Video, as it turns out, did not kill the radio star, because there are as many radio stations in Athens as there are in cities with twice or three times its population.

Language

The Greek You Already know

Even if we use the expression "it's all Greek to me" to signify our confusion or lack of understanding on a subject, in truth anybody who speaks English actually knows a lot of Greek, since much of the English language is derived from it.

To start, in Greek the word for "I" is "Ego" (e-GO). Freud notoriously used this Greek word to explain the conscious part of the self, and even today, we still use derivatives like "egotistical" and "egomaniac" to describe someone whose sense of self dominates his or her personality.

Another clear example of this influence is the Greek word for book, "biblio" (pronounced viv-LEE-o). It's where "the Bible" comes from, literally meaning "the book" and the word "bibliography," which is actually a compound word composed of two Greek works "biblio," meaning "book," and "grapho," meaning "to write."

All of the lingo we use for science, words like "mathematics," "chemistry," and "physics," all come from Greek, and the more you look back at the roots of many English words, the more you realize all of the Greek you already know and why those words mean exactly what they mean.

Here is brief look at some common English words and their Greek derivatives to help Greek seem...well, not so Greek:

- **Biology**

    Bios (life) + **logos** (to speak or to study) = **biology** (the study of life)

- **Anthropology** = study of people

    Anthropos = person

- **Zoology** = study of animals

    Zo = animal

- **Cardiology** = study of the heart

    Cardia = heart

- **Geology** and **Geography**

    Gei (earth) + **logos** = **geology** (study of the earth)

    Gei + **grapho** (to write) = **geography** (to write the earth)

- **Astronaut**

    Asteri (star) + **nautis** (sailor) = star sailor

- **Astronomy**

    Asteri + **onoma** (name) = naming of the stars

- **Astrology** = study of the stars

- **Philosopher**

    Philos (friend) + **Sophos** (wisdom) = friend of wisdom

- **Cosmopolitan**

    Cosmos (world) + **politis** (citizen) = citizen of the world

- "**Auto**," in Greek, means "this thing" and is the equivalent to the English word "it"

Autograph = thing you write

Automobile = thing (it) that moves

Automatic = thing that has it's own will (goes by itself)

- **Mono/poly** = the Greek words for one/many
- **Monogamous, polygamous**, etc.

(**gamos** = wedding)

Note: **monopoly** = **mono** (one) + **poli** (city) = one city (single owner)

- **Megalo/micro** = the Greek words for big/small

Mega-mall = big mall

Megaphone = **mega** + **phoni** (voice) = big voice

Megalith = **mega** + **lithos** (stone) = big stone

Microcosm = **micro** + **cosmos** = small world

Microbe = **micro** + **bios** = small life

Microorganism = **micro** + **organismos** (body) = small body

- **Neo/paleo** = the Greek words for new/old

Neolithic = **neo** (new) + **lithos** (stone) = age of the new stones

Paleontology = **paleo** (old) + **logos** = study of the old

- **Prin** (Preen)/**meta** = the Greek words for before/after

Prehistoric = **prin/pre** (before) + **istoria** (history) = before history

Metamorphosis = **meta** (after) + **morphosei** (change) = after the change

- "**Den**," in Greek, signifies negation when put in front of a word.

Comes directly into English, making the prefix "de-"

Decaffeinated = not caffeinated

Decentralize = not centralized

Decriminalize = not criminalized

Deemphasize = not emphasized

- The prefix "a," meaning a negative also comes directly into English.

Asexual = without sex

Amoral = without morals

Agnostic = **a** + **gnosei** (knowledge) = without knowledge

Apathy = **a** + **pathos** (feeling) = without feeling

Asymmetric = **a** + **syn** (together) + **metrikos** (measure) = not measuring together

Written language

A written language is something that many cultures don't develop for a long time, if ever. But with the help of the Phoenicians, the Greeks developed the skill very early on and English came to adopt and adapt much of the Greek alphabet. However, in certain circumstances, we replaced some of their letters with different characters, which can make reading Greek kind of confusing.

Here's a quick guide to the Greek alphabet and roughly how they translate into Latin characters:

Α	α	Alpha(1)	A (soft, like almond)
Β	β	Beta	V (like vinegar)
Γ	γ	Gamma	G (like golf, but more throaty)
Δ	δ	Delta	D (but with tongue, like "d" + "th" together, as in "this")
Ε	ε	Epsilon	E (like egg)
Ζ	ζ	Zeta	Z (like zebra)
Η	η	Eta	I (long, like feel)
Θ	θ	Theta	TH (like thing)
Ι	ι	Iota	I (long, like feel)
Κ	κ	Kappa	K (like kangaroo)
Λ	λ	Lambda	L (like long)
Μ	μ	Mu	M (like mom)
Ν	ν	Nu	N (like none)
Ξ	ξ	Xi	KS (like kicks)
Ο	ο	Omicron	O (soft o, like orbit)
Π	π	Pi	P (like people)
Ρ	ρ	Rho	R (like row)
Σ	σ(ς)*	Sigma	S (like song)

Τ	τ	Tau	T (like tiger)
Υ	υ	Upsilon	Y (as a vowel, like in shiny)
Φ	φ	Phi	F (like fish)
Χ	χ	Chi	CH (like school)
Ψ	ψ	Psi	Ps (like shops)
Ω	ω	Omega	O (hard o, like orbit)

*this version of (sigma) is used when sigma comes at the end of a word.

Notes: (1) These are the English names of the Greek letters. (2) The Greeks use an accent (') over at least one vowel in every polysyllabic word. The accent doesn't change the pronunciation of the vowel, but instead marks the syllable that is emphasized.

As you can see, in Greek, the vowels A, E, I, O, and U are all present and pretty similar with "Y" being a vowel as well. But the Greeks have no pure "u" sound (like "up"). Instead they have three vowels that sound like "ee," two that sound like "o," and an array of vowel combinations that produce different sounds, making spelling and reading quite difficult.

The consonants can be even trickier. For instance, the "B" sounds like a "V," and the "P" sounds like an "R." The "H" becomes a vowel, like a long "I," and the "w" becomes a vowel, like an "o." The "v" becomes an "n" and the "x" is pronounced something like an "h." The Greeks have a sound for "X" (like sex), but it looks like this, "Ξ" or like this, "ξ," in the lower case. Those are just a few examples, which might help to clarify or perhaps confuse you more about some things. Obviously, it just takes time and practice to learn them.

What is even more interesting is how and why the shapes of the letters, even some of the ones that we use today, came into being. Most of the written characters have a long and complex history of evolution, but in a few cases, the explanation is quite simple. The characters of the letters were drawn to mimic the shape of the mouth when that sound is being produced.

"O," or omicron, is the most obvious example. The simple shape of a circle is both easy to draw and clearly outlines the open mouth as it looks when that sound is being made. Not so different in appearance from omicron is "theta," which is written as "Θ" or "θ." The circle with the line in the middle illustrates the appearance of the mouth with the tongue present, when the sound of "th" is created. And finally, "phi," written as "Φ" or "φ" is the English equivalent for "f." Again the circular contour of the mouth is evident, but it is interrupted with a vertical line that represents how the teeth are used to create the breathy sound.

Some of those Greek characters passed over into English, some didn't. But even the word "alphabet" comes directly from Greek, with "alpha" being the first letter and "beta" being the second, so it's essentially like calling the alphabet the "abc's." One obvious question that arises for most people is why the word "alphabet" is spelled with a "ph" instead of an "f."

English spelling is one thing that irks almost every student learning the language, because it seems to be so arbitrary. But actually, in most cases, there is a logical explanation as to why a word is spelled a specific way and most of these seemingly strange spellings came about when people were first translating and transcribing Greek words using the Latin alphabet.

It's quite evident that there were and are certain inherent disparities between the sounds and tones used in the different languages. In other words, there are some sounds that we English speakers use that the Greeks don't, and vice versa. So, in many circumstances, the people writing down the Greek words in Latin were just doing their best to capture those unique Greek sounds using whatever Latin letters, or combination of Latin letters, they thought captured the sound best.

Notice how the percussive sounds of "P" and "F" are actually not so different from one another, and how many other sounds in the English language closely resemble each other, like "M" and "N and "D" and "B." The ancient Greeks also had some of those slightly different, yet similar sounding letters and the early translators probably chose to write that "ph" to represent the distinct Greek sound, as they heard it. What they heard for "Φ" or "phi" wasn't exactly a "P" or "F," so they tried to capture that sound and distinguish it by writing the "ph."

This is the reason why phonetic isn't spelled phonetically and why words like alphabet, philosophy, and telephone (which comes from Greek and literally means to send the voice) are written as they are.

Another good example of this is why the word school is spelled "school," instead of "skool." It's because the original word in Greek is "σχολείο." The Greeks have a letter for "K," being kappa, and "X," or "chi," which is pronounced something like "hee" (not like the English "ch," as in "church"). In order to capture that Greek "X" sound, the "ch" was used, probably with the intent of being pronounced phonetically, as a hard "c" (but not so hard as a k), followed by an h, in quick succession. Therefore, the "x" is translated to a "ch" and "sxoleio" became "school." (Plus many others like chemistry, chord, and character.)

Another questionable spelling is my name, Thomas. Why with "th" and not just a "t"? It's because in Greek, there is Τ (taff) and Θ (theta). Since we don't have a character for "theta" in English, the "th" is used to represent that sound. The original name was "Θωμάς" (which is pronounced Tho –MAS). We changed the pronunciation of the name, but kept the original spelling, as we did with many other words. Greek is the root for all the words that start with "psy," words like psychology, psychic, and psychedelic. They all come from the word "psychi," which means soul in Greek and is pronounced straightforward as "psee-hee." We just dropped that "p" sound, but kept the spelling as it was originally transcribed.

A Little bit of Grammar

In Greek, like in English, pronouns (he, she, it) are broken up into three main categories: masculine, feminine, and neuter. That much is simple. However, in Greek, like in all of the romantic languages, the adjectives describing those nouns change suffix depending on the sex of the object they are describing. So Greek isn't like English, where adjectives always remain the same, independent of their context.

For example, in English, yellow is always yellow, big is always big, and small is always small, no matter who or what the adjective is describing (i.e. a small girl, a small boy, a small cat). But in Greek, even if the word for small is "micro," that only applies to something that is neuter. When describing a boy, it becomes "micros," and for a girl becomes "micri," signifying gender within the adjective itself. Plus the articles before the word change as well, so there are six forms of the word "the" and another six forms of the word "a" or "an," which change depending on the gender and number.

Furthermore, in English, it's a basic rule that anything, which is not specifically male or female is considered an "it." But in Greek, this is not the case. Although most feelings, animals, and objects are considered neutral, there are also many "its," which the Greeks have assigned a gender to. And remembering which sex inanimate objects are makes Greek even trickier, because there is no definite rule dictating what is masculine and what is feminine. You just have to memorize them and speak accordingly. However, there is an interestingly subversive pattern that arises underneath what the Greeks chose to call male and female, and that pattern reveals a lot about what humans have traditionally considered to be masculine and feminine attributes.

For instance, the Sun, the wind and the sky are all male; while the Earth, the sea, and fire are all female. Love, beauty, art and truth are feminine, while war, anger, fear and pain are all masculine. This sexual dichotomy is ever present. Dogs are male. Cats are female. Life is female. Death is male. Water, the balanced, neutral entity is the only one of the four elements to be considered neuter and oddly, the moon, which has long been a sign of femininity, is also considered neuter as well.

So, as you can imagine, the Greek language is very difficult to speak grammatically, since there must be constant agreement between both gender and number, factors which cause the endings of words to change dramatically. But it goes even farther. Even the suffixes of proper nouns, like names, vary depending on their context. For instance, take a name like Giorgos. When people are speaking about the person, they would refer to him as "Giorgos." But, when they speak directly to him, they will address him as "Giorgo" and when they're talking about something that is his they say "Giorgou." So the ending changes, depending on how the word is being used (as the subject or the object or the possessive or an agent).

And what can further complicate one's understanding of the Greek language is that despite being so strict grammatically, Greek is actually very loose structurally. It is just as normal in Greek to say, "I am Tom," as it is to say, "Tom, I am." This makes aural comprehension quite difficult, since it can be tough to place where the noun or the verb is within a sentence. The word arrangement is rather fluid, so the same basic thing can be said using multiple and completely different word orders.

Plus, the Greeks have formal and informal ways of speaking. When you're talking to someone older than you, you're supposed to speak to that person as if they are more than one person, in the "you-plural" or "you all" form, to show your respect for them. As a result, it can be easy to inadvertently and subconsciously offend someone by either speaking or not speaking formally to him or her. You never want to disrespect your elders, but you also don't want to falsely assume and verbally project out loud that someone appears older than they are. And because the Greeks often use that you-plural form when talking to a single person, there are certain circumstances when it can be hard to tell if someone is speaking to one person specifically or addressing everybody generally.

On top of all of that confusion, the amount of expressions, euphemisms, and metaphors the Greeks use is uncanny. So even if you understand all of the words, you still might not be able to understand the meaning. Here is a look at some commonly used words, expressions and phrases to help you get a sense of how fluid and ambiguous the Greek language can be.

Useful Words

Neh and Ohi – The Greek words for "yes" and "no." This is something that can be confusing at first, because their word for yes (pronounced like "neh") sounds a lot like the word for "no" in many other languages. In most Western countries, no is basically no: in English (no), in Italian (no), in Spanish (no), in French (non) and in German (nein). All are simple, monosyllabic words that start with the same consonant, but of course the Greeks had to be different. Their word for "no" is "oxi" (O-hee), which is a bit odd because, unlike all of the others, it starts with a vowel and is polysyllabic, which basically means that it is easier to say "yes" than it is to say, "no" in Greek. This little mundane detail helps to explain a lot about Greek life. Why say "no," when it's so easy to say "yes"?

Parakalo (pah-rah-kah-LO) and **Euxaristo** (ef-har-ees-TO) – These are the Greek words for please and thank you. Euxaristo (thank you) means "good grace" and parakalo (please) literally means "before I call." But parakalo is not only used as "please," it is also used as the greeting Greeks say when answering the phone or replying to somebody, who has called their name. And parakalo is also used as, "you're welcome." So when someone says "euxaristo," you reply "parakalo."

Geia (gyee-AH) – is the Greek greeting, which literally means "health." They say it for "hello," "goodbye" and even for "cheers." I guess they use it so much because Greeks believe health is the most important thing and they're right. If you don't have that, then what do you have?

Ela (E-lah) – is another singular word that is used for different situations. It literally means, "come" and is used most frequently like the phrase "come on." But "ela" can also be used to mean "tell me" or "give it to me." For instance, when someone asks, "can I talk to you," you can respond, "ela."

Malakas (mah-LAH-kas) – is a widely utilized profane word that literally means "jerkoff" or "wanker." Although, it is not polite, the word is frequently used among friends with affinity, as well as to insult one another. Its connotation is softer than "a-hole," more like just "ass" or "jerk," and it's a word you will no-doubt here Greeks saying a lot. It's probably the most important Greek word to know. Learn when and how to say it right and you'll be well on your way to fluency.

Opa! (OH-pah) – This is a phrase used to express excitement. It has no definite meaning, kind of like "woohoo," "hurray" or "oops." Traditionally, it is used during dancing, but is also said as a vocal expression when something happens accidentally or surprisingly. For instance, if a Greek drops something, they'll say "opa" as they try to catch it.

-aki (AH-ki) – is not a word, but a suffix that you can attach to the end of almost any noun to add the connotation of that object being "little and cute." It's like adding "y" in English making dog into doggy. So "skilo" (dog), becomes "skilaki," and "paidi" (child) becomes "paidaki." The Greeks use it for everything, even names (Dimitris = Dimitraki). So, if you don't understand the language it can sound like they're constantly saying "aki, aki, aki, aki, aki."

Expressions

Some of the sarcastic expressions that the Greeks use appear to be completely nonsensical, and to a foreigner, their translations can be sidesplitting. Here is a list of sayings and what they literally and figuratively mean.

"Writing someone (or connecting them) to your balls"

The Greeks use this one a lot. It means that somebody is ignoring you, not responding or not paying attention to what you're saying.

"Two birds are sitting and knitting a sweater"

Nobody knows why the birds are knitting a sweater, but it's something they say to somebody, who is daydreaming and completely in their own world.

"You want me to smell my nails?"

It's a sarcastic expression used when somebody is asked about something they don't have the ability to foresee. If somebody asks, "Do you think it's going to rain next week?" The other person might reply, "do you want me to smell my nails?"

"Your mind and a pound"

It sounds like complete nonsense, and is said to somebody who is saying just that, nonsense, or something that is unrealistic. You might say the phrase to somebody who says, "If I can just think of one good idea, then I can sell it and get rich."

"This place is at devil's mother"

It's the Greek equivalent to "it's in the middle of nowhere," to describe a place that is far away.

"Catch the egg and give it a haircut"

This is one of my personal favorites, because it sounds so random and ludicrous. But that is what it is used for. You say it in response to someone, who is talking about something that is seemingly impossible to do.

Unspoken Language

There are also many things the Greeks say without actually saying anything at all. All cultures use nonverbal cues and the Greeks have their own versions of nodding the head for "yes," shaking the head for "no" and insulting with the middle finger.

Instead of nodding and shaking, the Greeks simply tilt their heads downward for "yes" and backwards for "no." Sometimes they don't even move their head at all. If they raise their eyebrows and make a clicking sound with their mouth, that also means "no." At first, it can be confusing because the actions are so subtle, you might miss them and think they're ignoring you if you don't pay close attention.

Finally, the Greeks do also use the middle finger as a sign of disrespect, but the real Greek insult is the "open hand." In the old days, the imprint of a painted hand on a door signaled a house of prostitution. So if you extend your open palm toward someone, it's the equivalent of saying "f-you." But like the word "malakas," which isn't always used to offend, "the hand" can similarly be used while joking among friends.

Chapter lessons on communication:

- Speak loudly. It helps to get your point across.
- Use single words and simple phrases to express very complex ideas (sometimes saying less says more)

- Use many words and complex phrases to express very simple ideas (sometimes saying more says less)
- Learn to say the same thing in a number of different ways (there are lots of words, use them)
- Use colorful metaphors and comparisons, because sometimes "the figurative" more clearly portrays "the literal."
- It's possible to carry on multiple conversions simultaneously at the same table.
- It's ok to yell, but always be polite about it.

Religion and Politics

(Two topics usually forbidden at the dinner table.)

Religion

Although Greeks are famous for the 12 deities living on Mount Olympus, they have embraced monotheism, as much of the world has. Christianity is by far the most prominent religion in Greece, with Orthodox being the denomination. Like most Christian nations, the Greeks have churches dotting every little community. The structures hold none of the grandiose splendor of Catholic Cathedrals, but hold a quaint beauty in their simple boxy shape, which is often capped with a dome on top.

However, the modest, no frills exterior is merely a façade for the lavishness inside. The interiors of the churches are adorned wall to wall with elaborate woodcarvings, vibrantly colorful paintings, and enough gold leaf to make you squint your eyes. This hidden, "beauty on the inside" concept is probably something the Greeks picked up from Muslim influence and is also evident in the way they build and decorate their houses.

No instrumental music is permitted in the church and the thickly bearded priests, who unlike Catholic priests are allowed to marry, drone on in monotone voices that echo throughout the columned interiors. Like many other European countries, most Greeks consider themselves to be religious, yet they seldom ever actually go to church. They might go for Christmas, Easter and the occasional wedding or baptism, but other than that, they hardly ever step foot inside a religious establishment. Instead, you might notice that many of them outwardly display their religious sentiments by wearing crosses, having a small shrine in their home and even regularly doing the sign of the cross three times whenever they pass by a church.

The Greeks hold the same sort of cynicism and distrust about religious establishment that most people do, as they often watch their holy priests, who are supposed to be caring for the poor, adorning themselves in fancy jewelry and driving around in brand new luxury cars. So the Greeks may be religious, but they're far from fanatic. They keep a healthy distance from righteous indoctrination and take their religion, like their alcohol, in moderation.

The bible is not preached politically nor is it taken very seriously by anyone but priests. This is partially because Greece is a land of philosophers and they have plenty of other ancient texts to read and discuss. But it's also because the nation is secure in its faith. Christianity is so overwhelmingly dominant in Greece that there is no real competition by any other faith to stoke defensive radical sentiments.

Personal character tends to be judged more by secular matters, like politeness, appearance and occupation, rather than outright religious piety. Shotgun weddings are normal, abortion is a health issue, and homosexuality is a personal choice. Nonetheless, religion does hold a significant place within the culture, being outwardly present and taught in public schools. Being baptized is a required rite of passage, but after that, your duties in the church are pretty much over until your wedding day.

One obvious contradiction to these monotheistic religious beliefs is the Greek conviction in astrology, superstition, and the use of charms (all things, which technically go against the church). If someone is interested in you, the first thing they will probably ask you, after your name, is what your horoscope or Zodiac sign is. It is a widely held belief that a persons' character is shaped by what stars they were born under, but some Greek women will even go so far as to qualify or disqualify, a potential suitor based on his astrological sign.

Belief in the "evil eye" is another example of mysticism within Greek culture. The evil eye is a widely held concept, which is embraced by many folk cultures around the world. It is the name given to a dirty look (usually cast out of jealousy, spite, dislike, etc.) that can supposedly create some sort of curse, or bring bad luck on the individual who receives it. To fend off that malicious energy, the Greeks use a small glass charm, which is blue and has a light blue eye on it. In Greece, you will see the symbol adorning many places, like the home and the car. It is also worn on bracelets and necklaces, put on key chains and is virtually impossible to miss, as it is sold in every souvenir and tourist shop.

Beyond that, Greeks similarly practice "knocking on wood" to try and stop a negative hypothetical from occurring. Horseshoes, pomegranates, and four-leaf clovers are seen as lucky, while encountering a black cat is unlucky. But besides those typical charms and hexes, the Greeks often interpret certain chance circumstances to be a predictor of some future event.

For instance, if your eye is twitching, that supposedly means you're going to run into somebody unexpectedly. If your hand is itching, then you will get money. If four people meet and happen to simultaneously shake hands diagonally across from each other, then one of the two people, whose hands are shaking on top, will get married. And if you put the last bit of wine in somebody's glass, whoever receives the wine will have good luck in money or love.

But what probably gives a deeper insight into Greeks and Greek life are those ancient gods from mythology that they are famous for. The polytheistic religion was not unlike many other old, traditional religions, which held beliefs of animism or the idea that all things have a spirit within them. The Ancient Greeks believed that the world wasn't made up of just one singular deity, but rather was comprised of a wide variety of gods, which each had control over their own specific domain. Those ancient gods supposedly interacted with humans face to face and on a very personal level. They could even mate with humans, from time to time, and create demigods, dynamic half-man, half-god characters, which actually serve as a precursor to the idea of Jesus Christ (being the son of a woman, who was impregnated by God through the Holy Spirit).

Here is a brief list of some of the most important Greek Gods and Goddesses and what they are typically associated with.

Gods of Mt. Olympus

Aphrodite	Goddess of love, romance, beauty
Apollo	God of music
Ares	God of war
Artemis	Goddess of the hunt, forest, wildlife
Athena	(The daughter of Zeus) Goddess of wisdom, war, and crafts
Demeter	Goddess of agriculture
Hephaestus	God of fire
Hera	(The wife of Zeus) Goddess of marriage
Hermes	The messenger of the Gods
Hestia	Goddess of the home and home life
Poseidon	God of the sea, storms, and earthquakes
Zeus	Lord of the gods, god of the sky
Hades	(Brother of Zeus) God of the underworld

The myths started out with just the twelve Gods of Olympus (and Hades), but as time went on more and more were added for each specific thing, as the gods reproduced and the stories became more elaborate. However, at the forefront, was always the mighty character of Zeus, who was considered to be "the king of the Gods" and supposedly "the father of man."

So in all actuality, it's no wonder that the Greeks were so easy and quick to accept Christianity. After all, it wasn't such a far stretch for them, since Christianity adopted many of their early beliefs: the Gods being in human form, a singular, all-powerful deity (Zeus = God), which is surrounded by lesser divinities (lower gods = angels), and is capable of having his own godly children (Athena = Jesus).

Philosophically, and like all religions, the idea of those gods didn't come out of nowhere. They came about to symbolize the observable, physical world. Greek mythology just took the natural forces, which are so evident in their environment and personified them into the image of humans. Essentially, the gods are just metaphorical representations of natural elements. They are a creative speculation for the "how" and the "why" of human existence.

The purpose of the gods was to simplify the complex world, to offer an explanation for otherwise inexplicable events and to provide answers to all the questions that humans couldn't and still can't answer. The gods' served to make the world seem more easily understandable. Zeus had his domain up above, controlling the heavens and the sky, while Poseidon ruled over the fluid world of the sea and the storms. Hades dealt with death and the underworld, and all together they contributed to events and manipulated the world to create this giant mess, which we call reality.

The Greeks even assigned gods to the inexplicable internal forces that influence humanity, like feelings. They had Eros, the god of love, and Dionysus, the god of drunkenness. Those ancient gods, like all gods, played a huge role in the minds of the people, and still hold a place in influencing the lives of Greeks today, predominantly in language. The Greek word for sun, "Illios" (pronounced EE-lee-ose) comes from the god of the Sun. The Greek word for north, "Boreia" (VOH-ree-a), comes from the God of the Northern wind that brought winter, and the Greek word for volcano "Iphaisteio" (ee-FES-tee-o) comes from the god of fire. The list goes on and on.

The Greeks also recognized early on the inherent duality of nature, the darkness versus the light (something that is ever present in Christianity as well). There was Zeus, the good god of the living, versus his evil brother, Hades, the god of the dead, and each deity is seemingly equipped with its own constructive and destructive capabilities. The sun brings life and makes the crops grow, but can also cause droughts and create deserts. You need water to drink, but you can also drown in it. The sea (Poseidon) can give you food, but can also eat you. Fire (Hephaistos) gives warmth, but can also burn you. So the gods' powers represented the ability of the natural world to positively and negatively affect humans.

As a result, the Greeks tend to approach the Christian God with the same sort of cautious reluctance they held for the ancient gods. It is necessary to stay in touch with the gods, to honor them, to feed them and to offer them sacrifices (in order to curry their favor and encourage the gods to, in return, provide what was needed for their survival). But you must also keep your distance from the gods, because if you get too close or try to challenge their authority, the gods can easily smite you if they please.

These natural dichotomies were given much attention, but nothing seemed to perplex the Ancient Greeks more than the age-old conundrum, which we are still struggling with today: free will versus fate. The Greeks recognized that there were certain things they could control and others they couldn't. So myths were often constructed to illustrate this conundrum. Even though the gods were depicted as being all-powerful, their relationship with humans was still very much represented as a two way street. The gods provided everything for humans, but humans could also influence their fate by courting the gods, using sacrifices and exhibiting certain behavior, which could give the gods more power. According to some of the legends, humans could even trick the gods from time to time.

Even today, the most advanced scientists and theologians (which is by the way a Greek word, theos = god + logos = study) are still wrestling with that same question the Ancient Greeks were asking thousands of years ago. Is the universe deterministic or chaotic? There is evidence suggesting that it is both and nothing seems to encapsulate this persistent enigma more vividly than the ancient Greek myth of Oedipus.

Oedipus is the tale of a child, who was prophesized to have the unfortunate fate of killing his father and marrying his mother. When Oedipus learns of his fate, he does everything in his power to stop it from happening, only to have his attempts ironically lead to the prophecy's fulfillment and that fate, which he had tried to escape.

Outwardly, the story seems to suggest that fate is fate and that we can't act against it. But the story also raises some more intriguing questions, which go unanswered. Was the prophecy merely self-fulfilling? In other words, would Oedipus have done the same thing had his fate been unknown to him? Or couldn't Oedipus have perhaps taken more drastic measures, like suicide, to prevent it? Either way, the clear lesson seems to be, not whether or not fate exists, but that any such destiny is up to the gods and is something, which is better to be left unknown to mortals.

Curiosity supposedly killed the cat and this sort of skepticism toward our innate human instinct, to want to know and control, is what has partially caused the Greeks to lag behind much of the modern world when it comes to certain innovations and developments. The Greeks proceed cautiously, both out of logical choice and out of fear that they might overstep their bounds and go too far. So despite how revolutionary and progressive the Greeks are in one sense, they remain highly traditional and old-fashioned in others.

Chapter lessons on religion:

- Be religious, but not fanatic.
- Religion should guide your life, not dictate it. The "rules" are more like guidelines.
- Symbolism should not be taken literally.
- Beliefs are different than facts.
- It's ok to practice and explore multiple spiritualities.
- Even if good luck charms don't work, there's no harm in having them ...just in case.

- There are some things, which are and always will be impossible for living mortals to know and understand.
- It's better to not know your fate.
- Beware of soothsayers and fortunetellers.

Politics

Greece has a parliamentary system with two main parties, one liberal democratic and the other socialist, along with a wide variety of fringe parties that run from communists to ecologists. For being the ones who invented democracy, Greeks have become awfully cynical about it. Voter turnout is extremely low and the sentiment during elections is unenthusiastic. To Greeks, voting has become a chore of choosing which candidate is going to steal from them next.

Until the mid-1970's Greece was governed by a military dictatorship and since then has always leaned toward the left. The public sector employees tend to side with the socialists, while the private sector with the liberal democrats. The socialists have held power for much of the time and the communist party consistently receives more than 10% of the vote during most elections.

With so many third parties fragmenting the results, it is often very difficult for one party to gain a clear majority and create a solid working government. Therefore, weak, coalition governments are usually formed, which break down rather quickly and regularly bring governmental business to a halt.

The discourse during political campaigns is focused predominantly on monetary and legal matters. Although the candidates' personal lives are often addressed, hot button social issues, like abortion and homosexuality, which tend to dominate the political discourse in the United States, seldom ever enter into the political discussion. The party platforms are based mainly on governmental procedure and economic philosophy, rather than social ideology. Each party has its own base of support, but party affiliation and allegiance are not strong. Therefore, in Greece, there is not such a deep political rift, which polarizes the population. Most Greeks consider all politicians to be crooks and would just assume not vote or vote for one of the smaller parties, than vote for one of the major candidates, whom they equally despise.

To put it plainly, most of the Greeks have simply lost faith in the system, and since there is such a large disconnection between the voters and the elected officials, the social dynamic has become shaped largely by a sentiment of "us vs. them:" we, the people vs. they, the government. The consequence of this strong political distaste is the persistent and widespread civil unrest that routinely occurs in the form of the protests, which primarily target the government and the police, and sometimes turn violent.

To vent their displeasure with almost anything, the Greek people will systematically stop working, the shops will close, all of the public transportation will grind to a halt and they'll take to the streets and yell. This sort of rebelliousness is just built into their culture and permeates every level throughout Greek life, large to small and starts at a very young age, even before students go to the university. It is not at all uncommon for high school and even middle school pupils to occupy their schools and lock all of the doors with chains in protest of whatever bothers them. As a result, public officials are forced to legislate extremely cautiously and quietly, with the constant awareness that their policies could create a serious backlash.

You'd think that this is the ideal situation for democracy, one which the government fears the people and therefore must act in their interest. But sadly, it is not. The politicians just subversively steal as much as they can with whatever time they can salvage in office, give away no-bid contracts to their friends and hide the money before anybody has a chance to notice it's gone. Most of those officials get away with it, scot-free. They might lose their position in government, but they seldom ever get prosecuted and usually end up with a small fortune. This is one of the problems with the Greeks. They are keen, which also means that they can be extremely crafty.

Greek politicians will seem so nice and polite to your face, but all the meanwhile they'll be stealing everything from you behind your back, and you'll never even realize what's happening until it's too late. In Greece, certain sectors, both public and private, together function as a big black market. Lots of business is done "at night," "under the table," and using "black money." Tax evasion runs rampant, and the government doesn't even know how to start to combat it, because almost everybody, including most of the government officials, is taking part in it.

There are certain legal mechanisms in place to try and stop tax evasion. For instance, absolutely everything sold in Greece, including a beer at a bar, must be issued with a receipt, and government inspectors routinely monitor this practice, doing undercover stings and levying huge fines upon those who violate the law. But this method of enforcement only works in established shops with storefronts, leaving all of the rest of the businesses, builders and contractors out.

One of the government's latest attempts to crack down on tax evasion is to use helicopters to fly over villas and assess the wealthy peoples' incomes based on their houses and property values. However, the Greek people are so sneaky that they are going as far as using camouflage covers to conceal their swimming pools.

This sort of shady business happens all over the world, and wouldn't be such a big deal if it weren't so widespread and if Greece didn't have such an enormous public sector to support. The power, the telephone, the Internet, and even a few of the major TV stations, plus most other utilities and services, are all government run or at least heavily regulated. This has resulted in large, centralized bureaucracies, rife with nepotism, corruption and frivolous spending, which have seriously hindered Greece's economic growth and prosperity. There is a joke in Greece about how the Greeks do business and it goes something like this:

The United States is funding a mission to go to Mars and they're interviewing some of the world's foremost scientists to help. After doing much research, they narrow it down to three candidates: a German, a Frenchman and a Greek.

The Americans go to the German first. They tell him how they've seen his work, how they're very impressed with him and how they'd like to potentially hire him to lead the project. They go through all of the details and explain to the German exactly what they want to do, and when they finally reach the matter of compensation, they ask the German how much he wants. The German thinks about it for a moment and replies,

"Gee, I don't know. For what you're asking, I'd say about a million dollars."

The Americans are a bit taken back by the very high initial offer and tell him,

"Well look. We still have some other people to interview, so thanks for your time, but we'll have to consider it and get back to you before we let you know for sure."

Then the Americans go to the Frenchman and do the same dance, telling him about the project and when it gets down to the money, the Frenchman says,

"Two million."

The Americans are even more surprised by that and reply,

"Two million? Well we just talked to a German and he said he could do it for one million. Now you're saying twice as much? We know that you're good and all, but we still have another guy to see, so we'll have to think about it and get back to you when we decide."

So finally the Americans go to the Greek, whom they're hoping might be able to do it for them for a bit less. They interview the Greek, explain the plan to him, and he seems very interested, and all seems to be going well, until they ask him how much he wants for the job and the Greek replies,

"Three million."

Now the Americans are in complete shock by that and respond,

"Three million? What? Are you crazy? We've already seen two other people, a Frenchman and a German. The Frenchman told us he could do it for two million and the German said one. Now you're telling us three million? That's crazy. Why? What are you going to do? Why would we need to pay you so much money?"

"Because." The Greek answers slyly. "It goes like this. You give me three million dollars. I'll take the three million and I'll give you back one million. Then I'll take one million for myself and give the German a million to do it!"

The scenario is quite outrageous, but the joke actually rings true with the way business and politics run in Greece. The public sector is absolutely massive, accounting for much of the country's employment and their procedures for working are riddled with nepotism, bureaucracy and red tape. A few families are in control of everything, including the major political parties. For basically the past thirty years, two men (Karamanlis and Papandreou) and their kin have occupied the seat of prime minister.

Getting pretty much anything done, from getting married to paying your water bill, can be a massive and expensive headache, because government offices and agencies are only open for a limited number of hours and are often disjointed and widespread. So citizens are left frantically running back and forth, from place to place, trying to figure out what they need, while talking to lazy, overpaid employees, who couldn't care less about what they're doing and have no incentive to actually do their job.

It's often angrily said amongst the Greeks that most of the public employees do nothing but sit around and drink coffee all day. It's not completely true, but up until recently, those employees enjoyed rich benefits. They worked short hours, had long vacations, and could retire early (sometimes after only twenty years) with a hefty government pension. This is actually the reason why little ever changes in the Greek political system, because the truth is that most Greeks actually have it pretty good and nobody wants that to change. In fact, most of the protests and strikes arise from the government trying to change something the Greeks don't want them to.

As I've already mentioned, Greeks can be pretty old school and traditional. They like to do things slowly and little by little, and the one thing that has helped them stay united and hold their identity together is that the population of Greece is mostly homogenous. Almost everybody in Greece is Greek, speaks Greek and is Christian. So there is little to be debated on that front since they're all facing the same way.

As a whole, Greeks are not typically patriotic flag-wavers and in fact, they'll usually be the first ones to make fun of and criticize their own fellow citizens. Sure, they are proud of their "Greekness," but they're not so nationalist. Local or regional alliances often trump patriotic sentiment and play a bigger role in their lives. After all, it was only fairly recently (in the 1800's) that Greece solidified into one nation and after the Second World War Greece was internally divided by a bitter civil war between leftists and governmental backed rightists. The right wingers eventually won with the support of outside forces (the US and UK) and even though the resulting military dictatorship has since been replaced, the wounds of this conflict haven't completely healed and elements of those extremist forces are still present in Greek society today.

So there are plenty of rivalries within Greece, like Athens versus the northern city of Thessaloniki, and in sports, there is no bigger rivalry than between the two Athenian teams Panatheinaeikos (pah-nah-thee-nah-ee-KOS) from the central Athens and Olymbiakos, from Piraeus, the port in the south of the city. These localized rivalries are a direct reflection of Greece in ancient times, when it was not a unified nation, but divided into city/ states. (Athens, Sparta, Troy, etc.)

However, since Greece's acceptance into the European Union, a large influx of immigrants have begun to flood in from neighboring countries, because Greece, being the farthest country to the south and the east, represents somewhat of a gateway into Western Europe. The Greeks can sometimes act like thieves when it comes to commerce, but most likely the thieves trying to pick your pocket on the streets are immigrants. Petty theft and even full out house and automobile robbery have become very common. So as I said before, in Greece, this is something you have to be extremely careful of. Everything must be locked, watched, or held onto, or it will disappear. And that is exactly what the Greeks fear will happen to their identity, as well, if they are not careful.

As a result, this new wave of immigration has started to stoke some of those nationalist sentiments, as the Greeks feel more and more threatened and seek to protect their country and their "Greekness" against the many cultures flooding into their native land. This has resulted in racist attitudes, widespread discrimination and violence against foreigners, particularly from Albania and the Middle East, who have come in the greatest numbers.

The negative feelings have a bit to do with a certain human psychological complex of racial superiority. The Greeks sometimes think they're the best because of something their ancestors did thousands of years ago. Sometimes they take too much pride in their history, which blinds them to the current situation their country is in. However, the intense xenophobia is mainly just a defense mechanism triggered by the fear of losing their unique culture, which they have struggled so hard to hold onto.

Throughout their history, the Greeks have watched their country get trampled on by foreigners from other lands. Mostly, it was the Turks for those four hundred years. But more recently, the Nazis invaded Greece during World War II and caused unspeakable suffering and more than three hundred thousand deaths. That's a lot of people in its own right, but it's even more of a tragedy for a country as small as Greece.

If you're a tourist from the West, you have nothing to fear and will probably never even notice it. The Greeks are more than happy to accept your money and share their beautiful country and way of life with you for a while. But that racism is very real and very dangerous, as it is in many other countries housing a large number of immigrants.

To protect themselves and in the spirit of the ancients, the Greeks still have a large and active military, even though they are not at war. Every male is obligated to complete six to twelve months of compulsory military service, which they must complete before they can legally be hired for a job. The military charade seems a lot like a show of muscle toward their perpetual rival, the Turks, whom they've had an ongoing spat with for years over the island of Cyprus, which the Turks invaded and currently occupy one third of.

Both countries constantly keep soldiers at their small, common border, guarding against attack and watching each other with a suspicious eye. From time to time, the two countries increase the tension by crossing into each other's waters, while doing research, military exercises or just by getting lost, and the comedy of it is that usually these disputes arise over invisible borders in the water and tiny islands, which are nothing more than a couple of rocks sticking out of the sea.

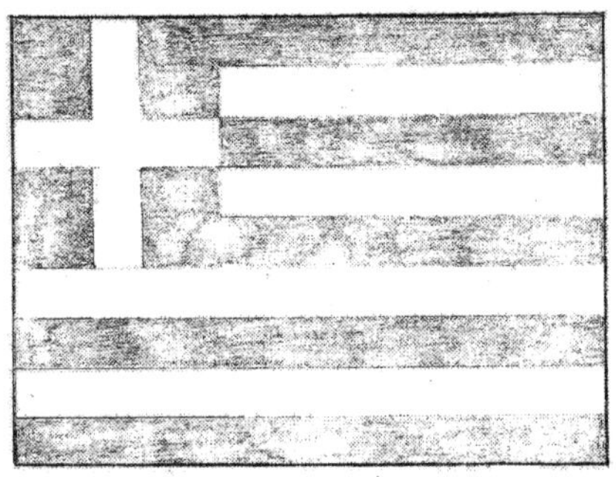

Still, the fear of foreign occupation remains, mainly in the older generation, and in fact there is a pronounced generational gap between those elderly, who hold memories of hard times during the war, and the Hollywood, pop-culture, influenced youth, who are trying to space themselves from the same heritage their grandparents fought so hard to keep alive. But Greeks are Greeks, no matter what their age. They may be urban socialists, but they also have a pronounced streak of independence within them. Even their beautiful flag of blue and white, symbolically means, "eleftheria i thanatos," meaning "freedom or death." The five blue stripes represent the syllables "e-lef-ther-i-a" and the four white stripes "i tha-na-tos."

There are many instances that the Greeks just want to do what they want to do, how they want to do it, and they don't care if it bothers anybody else. They'll play their music loud, even if they live in an apartment building. They'll speak Greek, even if they speak English. They'll carry their motorcycle helmets, instead of wearing them (just because it's a law to have one). They can't seem to form a straight line, because everybody wants to go first, and they drive like they own the road. Defensive driving is imperative in Greece and deadly accidents are common, many involving motorbikes, which can be very dangerous to ride, both in the narrow streets of the city and on the islands.

Police and riot police hold a large presence in the center of Athens, due to the threat of civil unrest. But overall, Greek authorities tend to be less invasive than authorities in many other countries. Unless you appear to be an illegal immigrant or you're doing something blatantly wrong, the police will probably never bother you for anything. For instance, on the highways, everybody speeds, yet nobody ever seems to get pulled over for speeding, and in most places, parking enforcement just doesn't exist.

Parking is an absolute free-for-all on the narrow streets and in the small lots, so people often just double-park and create parking spots everywhere and anywhere they can. Sidewalks don't really exist, because the sidewalks are used for parking, and since the sidewalks are always blocked, the pedestrians just walk in the streets. You can imagine the resulting traffic jams, which occur from all of this chaos and sometimes it's a wonder that anybody ever gets anywhere in Athens.

In Greece, there are no strict laws on drinking age or drinking in public, and even though smoking is technically banned inside restaurants and most public places, everybody still does it anyway. The non-smoking law is a rule that most Greeks and business establishments don't like, so they simply choose not to follow it. And what does the government do, upon getting ignored and so many complaints about the law? Instead of actually trying to enforce the law that they themselves passed, the government started making amendments to it, first allowing smoking in places that were such a size or had so many windows, until they basically again permitted smoking everywhere that they had originally banned it.

One unfortunate consequence of this "I do whatever I want" mentality is that nothing seems to function properly and the cities, parks and beaches around Athens are often littered with trash and cigarette butts, which can destroy the otherwise beautiful atmosphere. But the one thing that might piss you off about Greeks, on a more personal level, is that nobody ever seems to clean up after their dog. So when you're walking down the street in Athens or anyplace, you have to constantly watch out for the poop that is scattered everywhere.

Even though the Greeks live in small apartments, they love animals and pets, especially cats and dogs. There is a large stray population and the strays tend to gather around certain restaurants where the patrons feed them. But have no fear, because the strays aren't usually aggressive. They're oddly happy and healthy, taking part in the laid back way of life, relaxing and eating good food. There is no government program to deal with the strays and the Greeks don't seem to mind the extra mouths to feed because after all, there always seems to be plenty of food to go around. In truth, most of the Greeks believe that it is completely inhumane the way other countries gather up stray animals and "put them to sleep." Unfortunately, there are some bad apples in the Greek bunch, individuals, who have taken it upon themselves to try and help control the animal population by putting out poisoned food, which the animals innocently eat.

So, despite being rather socialist, Greece is overall very free. There are fewer civil arrests, per capita, than in the United States, which tends to prosecute people and lock up citizens for petty crimes, like possessing an open container of alcohol and public indecency. Since guns are virtually outlawed in Greece, except for the army and the police, violent crime is mainly limited to riots and fistfights, mostly between hooligans at soccer (football) matches.

On the other hand, illicit drug laws remain rather strict, since a good portion of Europe's drug supply comes through Greece on it's way north and west. Jail can easily be avoided by knowing the right people or simply by paying a hefty fee to forgo your time. However, if you're a foreigner and you do actually manage to do something stupid enough to get the police's attention, watch out because there are no equivalent laws to "habeas corpus." If you don't have the money or the sway to get yourself out, it is possible to be held in jail indefinitely, without any formal charges being pressed.

But all in all, if you mind your own business and watch your wallet, you'll have few problems integrating in Greece, because Greeks are international and liberal, both politically and socially, especially when considering their location near their extremely conservative neighbors in the Middle East.

Chapter lessons on politics:

- Democracy isn't perfect and needs to be protected, because it's fragile.
- Don't trust anybody, especially politicians and bankers. No matter what they say, they're all self-interested thieves.
- Take as much as you can from the government, but pay as little tax as possible.
- If you're going to be a thief, know how to steal (what to steal, who to steal from and when)
- If you don't like something, use your voice to complain about it.
- Protest, even if nothing changes.
- Love your country and be proud of your heritage, but also be its toughest critic.
- It should be the people vs. the government, not the people vs. the people.
- Practice evolution, as well as revolution. You must be adaptable because change is inevitable, but caution must be taken both ways. Sometimes moving too slowly can be as bad as moving too fast.
- Do what you want to do (within extremes). Freedom is a right granted only to those who exercise it.
- Know the right people and whose hand needs to be greased.
- Be nice to animals.

Family Life

Family life plays a central role in Greek life, as it does in most cultures. But first off, I must clarify that when I say "family" in Greece, I don't just mean the nuclear family, I'm talking about a vast network of extended family, plus the many close, personal friends, which surround a Greek individual and affect everything from their selection of a mate to choosing their children's names.

Typically, most Greek families are big and stay relatively close together, both geographically and emotionally. So when there is a family party, it's a real party. It's not just a few people stiffly sitting around a table. It's a place packed with a fringe of relatives from both sides of the family, loudly talking and stuffing themselves full of food and drink all day. There are usually plenty of kids running around and playing, babies being passed around, cousins, aunts and uncles, nieces and nephews and in many cases, a lot of them all have the same name. So when somebody's name is called, there is likely to be a clamor of four or five people turning their heads to respond.

Common names are typical in many cultures, but it's especially evident in Greece and there's a good reason for it. It's because most Greeks abide by the tradition of naming their offspring after one of their parents. Therefore, almost everybody in Greece shares a common name with at least one of their grandparents, if not some of their cousins and other family members as well. The convenience of this, as a stranger, is that you really only need to learn a handful of names, because when in doubt, you can just assume that a guy's name is probably something like Dimitris, Panayotis, Ioannis, Iorgos, or Nikos, and that a girl's name is either Maria, Elena, Ioanna, Christina or Katerina.

As I mentioned in politics, Greece is filled with nepotism, people doing favors for friends and family, and this dictates much of Greek life. Many businesses are family run and operated and most individuals will secure their job either directly or indirectly from the help of a family member. Not only is this nepotism a result of familial favoritism, it also has to do with Greek issues of trust. The Greeks don't trust anybody and because of their history, Greeks tend to be quite skeptical of outsiders. This makes it very difficult, if not impossible, for a stranger to get into the system without having the help of somebody who is already "in" and willing to vouch for them.

Amongst themselves, the Greeks are very open and generous. They shower each other and their family with elaborate gifts on any occasion and the parents will, in many cases, provide unbridled monetary support to their children for much of their lives. By many people's standards, Greek children are flat-out spoiled, because they are perpetually adorned with any and every luxury that their parents, grandparents, and relatives can afford. It is not at all uncommon for Greek children to live off of their parents and at home into their late twenties and thirties. There is no such, "you're on your own as soon as you're eighteen" mentality.

This lifestyle is as much about convenience and necessity as it is about choice. Since most Greek students study for many years and at universities close to home, it makes sense economically, because of the high cost of living. It makes sense for the children to just continue living at home and commute, and it's usually just as well for Greek mothers, being the offspring-attached, monarchal queens of the family they are.

Greek families are matriarchal. Although the men hold most of the control over income, business life and external affairs, when it comes to the home and the family, what the woman says, goes. To say the least, Greek mothers can be a bit controlling and can be what we modernly refer to as "helicopter parents," hovering around their children and trying to have a hand in every aspect of their life. This predominantly entails keeping their children fed and safe no matter how old they are, but it also affects their social lives and career choices as well.

Of course, the overbearing care and constant attention is only a result of motherly love, but it can also cause a substantial amount of tension in a Greek's life, since the smothering never seems to stop, even when the children grow up, get married and have children of their own. And it's not just the fault of the mothers, because the children often enable it to happen as well. Most Greek men are complete "momma's boys," doing and following whatever their mother says, much to the chagrin of their wives.

There is a generous tradition in Greece that the parents give their child and their spouse a house for their marriage. This usually means that the parents bequeath some piece of their real estate for the newly weds to live in. It's a great way to pass on inheritance and seems like the perfect foundation for a new relationship to start on. But there is often a catch and that catch usually is that the house or apartment is very near to the parents, if not in the same building. In fact, it is very common in Greece for married children to live in the apartment either directly above or below their parents.

Naturally, this works out perfectly for the mothers, since they can continue to keep an eye on their offspring.

But that enormous gift, which is helpful when first married, can quickly turn into an issue of contention for the couple. The lack of independence and privacy can be frustrating and the matriarch's influence can be downright suffocating. There are just some things, like what you do at night and when you come home, that you don't want your mother or mother-in-law to know, and there are other things that you just want to accomplish alone, without the help of others.

So, as with everything, close ties to their extended family present a situation of give and take. The grandparents can easily help out with little things and aid in the raising of their grandchildren, but they can also provide a perpetually irritating source of criticism, which their children must constantly endure from a close range.

Because of these tightly knit family relationships and the proud cultural heritage, a predictable trend of Greeks marrying Greeks arises and prevails as a standard. Cross-cultural marriages do occur but is somewhat rare in Greece. It's not simply because of their unique language, lifestyle, morals and the fear of foreigners. It's the sum of all of those things, which has created this idea that "Greeks are supposed to marry Greeks."

Greek mothers will quickly find and point out the flaws in any potential mate, even Greeks, as no man or woman will ever be, at first, considered good enough for their child. But beyond that, it doesn't matter if you're wealthy, good-looking or even a prince, if you're not a Greek, you'll be immediately disqualified and face the bitterest of opposition. They'll degrade you and your country. They'll point out all of the reasons why it can't and won't work, why Greeks are like this and why foreigners are like that, and why marrying a Greek is just better and easier for everyone. Some of their dissenting opinions will be valid, rational and even justified, but most will just be fodder from the fear that their child might make a mistake, get hurt or do the seemingly worst thing a Greek child can do to their mother, move away.

But in the end, Greece is a land of lovers and if all of that obstruction, fighting and complaining can't deter the will of the couple, then the family will ultimately concede and allow true love to prevail. It's almost like a test, an initiation and a rite of passage that all couples (even Greeks) must endure to prove they are strong enough together and that their feelings are for real. Because if you stick it out, put up with it and maintain your integrity throughout all of their defiance, then their guard will come down and you will be graciously and wholeheartedly accepted into the family. And once you are in, you're in. That's the end of it. All of those past discretions are water under the bridge and you become part of the family, one hundred percent.

So in Greece, as in all places, family defines one's character, solidifies one's identity and plays a most important role in shaping the development of an individual.

Chapter lessons on family

- Keep your family close, but not too close.
- Recycle names over and over again. It's one of the most sincere ways to express admiration and show respect for your elders.

- Listen to your parents, but don't always do what they say.
- Mothers bare the burden of all humanity (past, present and future), but they are not perfect, so don't expect them to be.
- Children need love, but they also need space to grow, so don't smother them.
- Blood is thicker than wine. Forge your own path, but always remember who you are and where you came from.
- It's ok to spoil your children and grandchildren...a little bit.

Social life

As you have probably already figured out, almost everything in Greece is social. So here is a closer look at what Greeks do in that time between going for coffee and going to the beach.

First off, punctuality is not one of the Greek's strongest suits. They're not like the Germans or the Swiss, whose trains run consistently and obsessively on time. Greek life runs on Greek time, with a delay. This is something you just have to get used to and expect, because otherwise you'll be constantly frustrated by their tardiness.

If your appointment is for three, it probably won't happen until at least three-twenty. If a party is supposed to start at ten, nobody will actually show up until eleven or eleven thirty. If somebody tells you they'll be there in half an hour, expect them in an hour. One minute easily becomes five. Five minutes becomes fifteen. "I'll call you tomorrow" means, "I'll call you sometime next week," and if they actually say, "I'm going to be a little late," it means they're going be really late. They can blame it on the heat or the traffic or the parking, but it is just a fact of life and this delay carries over into their everyday routine.

Lunch is not at noon, it's at two, and dinner is not at five or six, it's at nine or ten. The Greeks don't normally go to bed before eleven or twelve, and if they're going out to a club, they probably won't even leave to go until one or two in the morning. This procrastination is merely a symptom of their laid-backness. They kick back, relax and wait around all day until the absolute last minute. Then they freak out and try to go someplace, or do something haphazardly, when they could've been preparing all day. So contrary to the otherwise chilled out lifestyle, most business tends to be done in a frantic rush. It's zero to a hundred, as Greeks always seem to get caught one step behind at their own behest, and have to hastily make up for all of that time they just spent leisurely drinking coffee.

But even if promptness isn't widely practiced, politeness is. So although it is somewhat of a custom to be late, the Greeks still always apologize for it. It doesn't matter who you are or how much money you make, good manners are what matter most, because manners are seen as a direct reflection of one's self, one's family and one's upbringing. There are many good reasons to be late, and even rich or poor, but there is simply no excuse for being rude. And I'm not talking about eating with the correct silverware or knowing proper protocol, just basic decency, like saying, "please" and "thank you," and being respectful to your elders. If you practice these common courtesies, you should have no problem integrating into any social situation.

As a whole, the Greeks are warm like their weather, and they expect the people they're with to act with that same sort of jovial lightheartedness and generosity that they do. They like to be entertained and laugh out loud, so they consider most foreigners, especially northerners, to be "cold" if they don't express their feelings outwardly and openly. Probably the worst thing you can do socially, besides being rude, is to be silent or do nothing and appear emotionless (acting like a plant, as the Greeks say).

You should speak with animation, have conviction and be passionate. It doesn't matter what you're talking about, it matters how you say it, because the Greeks want to see your humanness. They want to know where you stand and if they can't see it visibly, then they'll probably find you perplexing, strange and even boring. In Greece, it's better to be angry than it is to be indifferent, because at least anger shows something about your character. Indifference is just confusing.

The Greeks love to talk. They love to go out together, to have fun and of course, to drink. But they tend to drink in moderation. They'll enjoy beer or wine everyday with lunch and dinner, but they seldom ever go out and get really drunk, not like the English and the Americans do. Getting completely blitzed is actually looked down upon, because it's seen as childish and irresponsible, and it reflects poorly on one's self control.

Like most cultures in the modern world, Greece has become enthralled in media and the celebrity culture, which has shaped their style and social attitudes. Despite being such a small country, the Greeks have an extensive array of media, both broadcast and print. Much of their television, movies and music are imported from America and abroad. But the Greeks have also produced a wide variety of popular programs and music, which has, in turn, spawned a domestic fame culture, complete with sleazy tabloid magazines that track the lives of their rich and "famous."

However, since Greece is so small, it's really not that difficult to get recognized or to end up in one of those magazines. Athens is sometimes referred to as "a village," because everybody seems to know everybody within certain circles. So when flipping through the thick Greek tabloids, it can seem kind of comical (and quite vain) to see the many candid and posed snapshots of seemingly random people printed on the same page next to A-list, Hollywood celebrities.

Even though a certain Greek "star" might be a household name in Greece, most of them actually don't make that much money and seldom ever make the jump abroad into larger markets. They always remain the equivalent of what might be considered a local or regional act in bigger countries. But in our attention-desperate world, I suppose it's better to be known by a few than unknown by all. Nonetheless, the Greek idea of what "rich and famous" is has certainly become somewhat demented by "the big fish in a little pond syndrome."

This resulting "I am special and can do anything" mentality has led many Greeks to become snobby, especially ones in their youth, who often have a bloated sense of ego and a mind filled with delusions of grandeur. They all seem to think that they're somebody and that what they're doing is something great, even if they're nobody and they aren't doing anything. They'll still wear designer clothes and drive luxury cars to project the image that they are. It all comes back to that theatrical idea of dynamic personality. It doesn't matter who you really are, it only matters who you appear to be.

I already mentioned that much of the population works in the public sector, but other than that, restaurants, retail stores and shops account for much of the rest of Greek employment. Even with the introduction of corporate chains, big box stores and supermarkets, there are still a lot of "mom and pop," privately run businesses, which occupy most of the storefronts throughout the cities. Business has certainly changed in the modern world, but because of proximity and heavy traffic, most of the time it's still easier and a lot quicker, in Greece, to just run down to your small neighborhood store and get whatever single item you might want to pick up. In other words, there is still a butcher, a baker and a candle shop maker.

One important aspect of Greek life is the "periptero." A periptero is essentially a kiosk, which you will see located on almost every street corner and square through every city and small town. They are open late, some even twenty-four hours and are essentially small, reliable, corner stores on every block. It's the place you go to pick up cigarettes, newspapers, magazines, candy, beverages, as well as pre-pay cards for your telephone and certain standard forms you might need for governmental business.

Periptera were originally created to employ war veterans and have turned out to be a very convenient aspect of Greek life. What is nice, both as a resident and a tourist, is that prices of most commodities are regulated by the Greek government, meaning that stores can only legally charge a certain amount for items. So you don't need to worry (too much) about being price gouged or ripped off on basic items, because you know that a bottle of water can legally only be so much, regardless of location. The same goes for most items in the supermarket and this allows smaller stores and chains to remain competitive.

No supermarkets are open twenty-four hours, by government regulation, and the store hours for privately owned shops are coordinated so that some nights during the week they are open later than others. The supermarkets and large chains are open regularly from morning until night, Monday through Saturday. But the Sabbath is still holy in Greece. The tourist shops and restaurants will remain open, but all of the box stores and supermarkets are closed on Sunday. This is nice for worker purposes, but inconvenient if you need something.

On the other end of the economic spectrum is the "lykei agora" (the popular market or people's market). This is a weekly farmer's market, which each local area hosts on one their main streets. The lykei agora is the best and most convenient place to pick up fresh fruits and vegetables directly from the farmers that grow them. You can get whatever vegetables happen to be in season, plus eggs and fish, and even clothes and household supplies from a little bazaar that often accompanies it.

Prices at the lykei agora are cheaper than the supermarket and the quality and atmosphere are unbeatable. It's pure capitalism, as Adam Smith described. Each farmer brings his or her products to the market and the prices aren't set. They openly fluctuate throughout the day, depending upon the quality, supply, demand and competition. If you wait until later in the day, the selection gets a little picked over, but you can also pick up some real bargains off people trying to get rid of whatever product they have left. Vegetables don't have a shelf life, so vendors do what they must to sell their product. The lykei agora is one of the only places in Greece where they don't issue receipts (recently a law was passed which states they must, but they still don't), so obviously checks and credit cards are not accepted.

Overall, cash is still king in Greece. Lots of restaurants (outside of tourist places) don't take credit cards, because it's a hassle and it leaves a paper trail, making tax evasion more difficult. Surprisingly, even though the government is drowning in debt, private citizens themselves tend to be rather fiscally responsible and are very wary of credit and loans. Most Greeks equate debt to the loss of one's sovereignty. So, as you travel throughout Greece, you will see lots of buildings, which sit unfinished. That is mainly due to lack of funds for a project to continue. The Greeks don't mind doing things at a slow pace, so they will repeatedly stop construction of a building again and again and build it incrementally, as they acquire the liquid funds (as opposed to taking a loan or a mortgage from the banks, which they despise).

As I stated at the start, climate has a large affect on lifestyle. Besides some earthquakes, the sun is really the Greeks' only nemesis and that celestial body is what shapes much of the Greeks' behavior. They build their houses out of concrete, not only because they have plenty of rock to work with, but also because the cement gives them better insulation against the sun. They paint everything white and the larger buildings can even hold the cool of the night throughout the day. Also to combat the heat, there is a siesta period every day in the middle of the afternoon, when the sun is at its strongest. Some of the shops and restaurants will even close during those government mandated quiet hours. No building or loud noises are permitted between 2:00-5:00 p.m. each day.

That's one aspect of life that the Greeks do take seriously: down time. Saying that "they work to live" is a bit of an understatement, because, in Greece, vacation is not seen as a luxury. It's a right and a necessity. At no time is this more evident than during August, when most of the population goes to the islands and Athens basically becomes a ghost town. During that time Athens (outside of the tourist areas) becomes a bit post-apocalyptic. There is nothing happening, no people on the streets, very few stores and restaurants open and most shockingly, no traffic. You can actually cruise down highways, which are usually like parking lots and you can drive to places in five minutes that at any other time of the year will take you at least a half-hour.

The peak of this summer exodus is around August fifteenth, which is a national holiday and happens to be the "nameday" of "Panagiotis" and "Maria," two of the most popular Greek names. The Greeks will find pretty much any excuse to party and "namedays" present a good reason to celebrate. "Namedays" are exactly what they suggest, a day to celebrate your name. The specific days of the year are usually based on an important date (birth or death) in the life of a patron saint with that name. Something similar globally is the celebration of St. Valentine's Day (February 14) or St. Patrick's Day (March 17) in America, when people celebrate those saints and what they supposedly represent.

Namedays are celebrated in Greece by anyone (and everyone), whose name coincides with that day. It's something like the celebration of a birthday, as the custom is to give that person presents and to go out. But in Greece, namedays usually tend to be bigger celebrations than birthdays, because so many people have the same names and thus celebrate on the same day. And, contrary to the customs in many countries, it is a generous Greek tradition for the person, whose nameday it is, to personally pay for and treat everybody who they choose to take out.

Education

Like many other things, the Ancient Greeks were the architects of education and much of the world still follows their model fairly closely today. Art (music and literature), science (biology and chemistry) and physical education were all on the ancient curriculum, which focused on creating a well-rounded individual, who could be adept at many things. Physical strength was very important back in those days, in case there was a need for war, so the children attended gymnasium (hence the word), which served primarily as a means for keeping the youth disciplined, healthy, and physically fit.

At gymnasium, the children learned specific skills in the form of games and exercises, which were useful in battle. But the Ancient Greeks also recognized that physical strength could only go so far, since muscles age and decay. They knew that the mind, when properly used, is a much more powerful tool than might. So heavy schooling was a standard and necessary to gain acceptance into the rich Greek social life. Literacy was essential, and the first thing they taught their children, from a very young age, was to read and write. Then they imparted upon them science for logic and art for imagination, the two crucial components for innovation.

Students back then were taught both formally and informally, very much like they are still taught today in Greece. Modern Greek students go to two different schools, usually a public school during the day and a "fraudestiria" in the evening. Both schools essentially teach the same subjects, however fraudistiria are private and less formal than their public counterparts. But unlike in Ancient Greece, where the informal schooling was free (from all of the philosophers roaming the streets), students of the fraudestiria today must pay a handsome fee to receive those more private lessons.

Overall, the educational system in Greece is very intense and demanding for the students. They are schooled from a young age in many advanced subjects, like philosophy, physics and foreign language. Since Greek is not a widely used language, they have taken it upon themselves to become bilingual and even tri-lingual as a standard. Almost everybody in Greece speaks English and to gain acceptance into universities and get many jobs, fluency in Greek and English, plus the working knowledge of another major world language, is required.

The public schools are free and the universities are cheap, but they are very difficult to get into, so a large number of students don't go or often choose to study abroad at some point in their education. This rigorous education system might sound perfect, but there is also a downside, because the highly demanding schools offer very narrow options and create an unfortunate byproduct. Many students, who are not so capable or driven by such high expectations, slip through the cracks and have created a somewhat radical youth subculture, which borders on anarchist and is sometimes prone to violence against authority.

Sexuality

One unflattering thing, which many other cultures credit the Greeks with inventing is homosexuality. The island of Lesbos, in Greece, is the place that lesbianism supposedly spawned from. And ancient writings from Greek philosophers, like Plato, don't help the stereotype, because the texts are often rife with blatant homosexuality, sometimes claiming that men were naturally better lovers and that part of enlightenment is moving beyond the instinctual nature of heterosexual relations. But obviously the Greeks didn't actually invent homosexuality, as the behavior is well documented in animals. Even if homosexuality is quite openly accepted in Athens and on some of the islands (like Mykonos), it is still shunned and violently oppressed in rural, more conservative areas of the country.

Beyond the gays, many Greek men have the typical Mediterranean "machismo" complex. They all seem to think they're Don Juan's, no matter how greasy or hairy their backs might be. So Greek boys and Greek men alike, even some of the married ones, will actively and openly pursue any modestly attractive women they come across. In response to this male aggressiveness, Greek women tend to be extremely defensive and standoffish, except only when in the company of known acquaintances and their closest friends. They're like that because the delusional and prowling Greek men take any tiny sign of interest as an open invitation.

Therefore, unless you know them, Greek girls keep to themselves and upon first impression, can come off as...well, to put it plainly...bitches. But really, it's only because Greek women are strong and not as submissive as women in some other cultures tend to be. Long before the woman's lib movement, since the time of Sparta, Greek women have been outspoken in their culture, demanding a place and a voice in a world, which is still very much male-dominated.

So if you're a woman visiting Greece, take note and watch out, because Greek guys might think you're flirting with them, even if you're ignoring them. On the flip side, if you're a man, good luck, because Greek women are a tough get. If a Greek girl is interested in you, you'll probably never even know it. In general, Greek girls will come across as sweet as candy to whoever they need to be, but be careful, because they don't take disrespect. If you cross them the wrong way, then hell hath no fury. It's all out psychological warfare. Greek women have the ability to go from hot to cold and back, before a man can even understand what he did wrong. They'll give you an earful and then shower you with praise. It's because feelings are probably the only thing the Greeks don't take in moderation. They are extremely emotional and feel every emotion to its extreme. Sadness is melancholy. Happiness is elation. Jealously is all consuming and anger is rage.

I guess it's just the hot-blooded Mediterranean in them that makes them so feisty, for better or for worse. Either way, the Greeks really feel whatever they feel, which, I suppose, is better than being numb, because that's no way of living or experiencing life at all. And that's a lesson we can all learn from the Greeks. No matter what you do, do it with your heart, whether it's working, playing, dancing, fighting or doing nothing at all. Relax. Take it easy. Empires rise and fall, like the sun. Youth and wealth will come and go. But if all else fails and life gets you down, just go for coffee. That'll pick you up.

Chapter lessons:

- Always dress to impress.
- Say "please" and "thank you." Simple good manners go a long way.
- Keep the Sabbath (or at least one day a week) holy and work-free
- Be fiscally responsible. Debt = Serfdom
- Don't buy everything from corporate chains. Sometimes "the little guy" can offer something better, more personal or more convenient.
- A well-rounded education is the best tool a person can have.
- Be bilingual, multicultural and worldly. It's good for your brain. But also, don't neglect your own customs and traditions.
- You don't need an excuse to have a party.
- Live life on your own time. Don't be a slave to the clock.
- Make vacation a priority.
- If you're a guy, go after that pretty girl (or guy)
- If you're a girl, watch out for guys.
- When in doubt, go for coffee.

Conclusion

"The only thing I know is that I know nothing."

That was something a wise Greek philosopher said five hundred years before Jesus of Nazareth was supposedly born. Yet that phrase still encapsulates the spirit of modern scientific thought. The more we learn, the less we seem to know. We've come a long way since then, but Socrates' words still ring as true as ever. He was a truly brilliant mind, who achieved immortality by doing nothing more than thinking and speaking his mind. All of the dead soldiers throughout history are no longer fighting, but those ancient teachers are still teaching.

Ancient Greece is what inspired Rome and the Renaissance. It influenced every major civilization that followed it, and throughout all the dark times in between, when civilization was in ruins, the great minds of the day could always look back at Greece and say (with actual, physical proof), "See. It can be done!"

Greece was the light in the darkness that proved humanity could be better, and those pillars of democracy still stand, even though many have tried to knock them down. All that we have today is built on top of the foundation they laid for us. As Sir Isaac Newton once wrote, "If I have seen a little further, it is by standing on the shoulders of giants." He was talking about Greeks. Really, it's all Greek, because as the Greeks so proudly say, "they were doing advanced algebra, while the rest of Europe was still swinging from the trees."

So hats off to the Greeks, because they did it first, but really, hats off to humanity for even doing it at all.

Greek, English, American, African, Asian. It doesn't really matter where you're from or where your parents were born, because people are people. The triumphs of the Greeks are the triumphs of humanity. We can all celebrate and be proud of what humans have collectively accomplished thus far.

Take these lessons from the Greeks and make them your own. Keep thinking and keep working, but not too hard. That's what the Greeks do and you can be Greek too, if you want. Because really, being Greek is not about speaking the language, drinking iced coffee or even living in the Mediterranean. Being Greek is simply a way of life and a method of thought.

Tom Simek was born and raised in upstate New York. An avid traveler driven by curiosity, he has studied a variety of subjects around the world, from the history of Europe to the medicinal plants of Northern Thailand and the geology of the Hawaiian Islands. He holds a Bachelors and Masters Degree in Music Composition, was a professor of music at the State University of New York at Purchase and has worked as a composer and performing musician throughout his adult life. When he's not quietly writing, reading, playing or studying, he likes to be outside, hiking, biking, surfing and extreme skiing. He currently resides in Athens, Greece, where he teaches English as a second language and lives with his wife, Lara, and their two cats, Lolly and Pop.

ΠΑΡΙΣΙΑΝΟΥ Α.Ε.
Διοίκηση - Γραφικές Τέχνες: Ιωάννου Ράλλη 21, 14452 Μεταμόρφωση
Τηλ. 210 28.55.183, Fax: 210 28.17.264, 210 33.06.880, 210 36.10.519

75106863R00057

Made in the USA
Columbia, SC
10 August 2017